DALLAS COP

VOLUME II

MORE THAN 400 TRUE SHORT STORIES

RAY DETHLOFF

Book cover design by The Book Cover Whisperer:
OpenBookDesign.biz

978-1-9772-4460-4 ISBN

This book is dedicated to the shocking number of Peace Officers that have died in the line of duty in the history of the United States. Since the first recorded in 1791, the startling total is now 26,032.*

*ODMP Officer Down Memorial Page as of 11/14/2022

FOREWORD

I want to thank you for your interest in reading DALLAS COP VOLUME II based on the presumption that you enjoyed reading DALLAS COP and returned for more. Originally, my thought was to use all of my material for one book, but I soon realized how voluminous that would be, hence the decision for this sequel.

DALLAS COP VOLUME II is teeming with more than 400 true stories, some long and some short. As such, there are far too many stories to be labeled with individual titles. These hundreds of stories are presented randomly, and include several uncanny or rare coincidences and observations, all culled from my career with Dallas PD 1990-2016. You never know what is coming your way next, except what I'm sure will be more enjoyable reading.

Ray Dethloff

A teenager was running from the police and hoofed it across a creek and into a field along the tree line. He didn't know that I had anticipated his direction of travel and was crouched down in the high grass waiting to pounce on him like a big cat stalking his prey. As he was running toward and almost upon me, I sprung into action. He was absolutely startled and turned to evade me. Several steps later I forced him to the ground from behind. He was wet and tired, and I was neither. I had difficulty handcuffing him because his wet and torn shirt kept getting in the way of his wrists. Stymied, I just tore his shirt off of him and cast it aside to complete the arrest, and I delivered him shirtless to the original officer.

I was told after his trial that he testified and was still angry than an officer had ripped his shirt off.

A sure way for a motorist to get a ticket during a traffic stop? By not even waiting for the officer to close his car door and shout back "What'd you stop me for!?" That happened several times.

Early Sunday morning not long after sunrise, I drove code 3 to a shooting. When I arrived and stepped out into the cold, it was eerily quiet. I found a dead male that had been shot in the back of his head lying on the edge of an apartment complex sidewalk with his eyes still open. I looked around for someone, anyone, but no one stirred. As the ambulance and another officer arrived, the sirens had caused a few curious people to step outside or open their front doors to watch. There was no lost love on the deceased victim; I was told that he was out there nearly every day dealing drugs.

I was working a DWI task force and was assigned to an unfamiliar area of Northwest Dallas. After a DWI arrest, with the arrestee sitting next to me, I had to look in my Dallas MAPSCO (an atlas of maps officers used daily for geographic orientation before there was GPS and computer-aided travel). The drunk prisoner asked me what I was looking for, and I candidly told him that I was needing to find out how to get to the county jail. "Oh, I can show you the way" was his reply, and he did.

An 18-year-old male was with a friend when they met up with a couple of guys who were "Bloods" gang members. Some epithets later, a scuffle began. The 18-year-old pulled the unknown gang member off his friend and held him until his friend could flee. At 12:30 AM, there was a knock on the door of the 18-year-old teenager's apartment. The mother answered. Outside, partly hidden from view, the gang member inquired "Is Kevin there?" The annoyed mother said that he was asleep, closed and locked the door, and walked back to her bedroom. She screamed when she heard a loud volley of three pistol shots just outside the front door. When she believed it was safe, she looked outside and saw no one. Her son was still sound asleep, never having heard anything. Had he been a light sleeper and answered the door, he would have in all likelihood been shot to death.

We used to have frequent calls to a probation office to arrest and transport those who had violated their probation. The one time that I didn't arrest someone there for a probation violation was when I arrested someone for APOWW, or Apprehension of person without warrant. This man had been on probation because he had stabbed his sister with a knife. Now he told his probation officer and the Psychologist that he had been having a dream every morning that he woke up with a knife in his hand, and then went to stab his sister. We told him that to be successful with his probation he needed proper medication to erase these thoughts. He agreed.   We handcuffed him and began our trip to the psych ward for his mental evaluation.

I did a favor for a nervous angst-filled woman by writing an Incident Report in case she ended up murdered so the assigned Homicide Unit detective would at least know a motive. To make extra money, she had been selling baggies of powder cocaine to drug users. That's what the buyers thought, anyway; they were really baggies of baby powder.

Early in my career, there had been a grazing pasture where an owner kept several miniature ponies at what is now LBJ Freeway and Plano Road. A suspect would come around in the late evening because he really liked ponies. Really, really liked ponies. Somehow, he realized that the miniature ponies were just the right height for bestiality. He was discovered "in the act" many times by the owners because there were many calls out there. He was always gone upon arrival by officers, except for one night when he was actually seen in the act and caught

by an officer after a short foot chase. Several of us who had

taken calls out there had to go and take a look at the weirdo as

he sat in the back of the police car, and his face was illuminated

by multiple intersecting beams from our flashlights.

D.A.'s in the USA will generally take a Cruelty to Animals

charge for this repulsive act.

After being out with her friends Saturday night, a girl

returned to her apartment early Sunday morning. As she was

distracted by going into her purse and getting her apartment

key, a suspect grabbed her from behind just as she was about to

unlock her door. He held a knife to her throat and told her to

"Go inside and Shut Up!" The girl had the presence of mind to

rebuff his demand, and said that she didn't want to go inside

because her little sister was asleep. The suspect then took her

back to her car and had her drive him around to several ATM's

to get some of her cash. This ill-fated plan was thwarted by the area ATM's computer network being down that morning, and no cash withdrawals could be made. The suspect had her drive back to her complex, then got her out of the car and took her through a hole in the fence that led to an adjacent apartment complex, naively his own. The suspect brought her inside his apartment. At knifepoint and sometimes at gunpoint, he forced her to perform oral sex and have intercourse with him.

In the hour around dawn while he was sleeping, she slipped out of his apartment unnoticed and called police. She believed that he was probably still inside his apartment, as it was still early Sunday morning. Some time had elapsed, and in case the suspect didn't come to the door, we wanted to be able to make an arrest. We drove to south Dallas and had an on-call Judge sign a personal and evidentiary search warrant from his home. We drove back and obtained a master key from the management office which had just opened. We surrounded his apartment, gained access, and arrested the naked, sleeping scumbag. The suspect didn't have any chance to get his pistol or knife, or to flee. The rape victim had told us that he had

spoken of leaving town that morning, and that he had boasted

of murdering a woman in California and of being on the FBI's 10

most wanted list. We did not confirm that.

Normally, most arrestees plead out, but this defendant

waited to plead out just minutes before his trial was set to

begin. He accepted 20 years without parole for admitting guilt

on three counts of Aggravated Sexual Assault.

A woman took her son to school and was home in 20 minutes.

The man that lived with her wanted to continue an argument

that he had started with her before she left, and told her that

she took too long and asked her where else she went. The

woman didn't like being interrogated and pestered and told him

that she was "tired of this shit!" She knew from previous

experience that he would be violent, but she still told him that

she was calling the police. The man pulled the phone cord from

the wall and exclaimed "You ain't calling nobody!" then pulled the screaming woman to the floor by her hair. He straddled her

and punched her in the mouth giving her a bloodied, swollen

lower lip. She managed to fend off and block 4 or 5 more

punches, and then squirmed enough beneath him to slip away.

The suspect was not at the location despite my quick arrival.

The woman had difficulty breathing because she was crying and

hyper-ventilating so badly, wheezing and needing to take deep

breaths. She needed several minutes to calm herself so that

she could speak to me for the report.

A mother called police because her 36-year-old son had been

drinking and would not leave her house to go home. We found

him lying on a bed naked wearing nothing but pantyhose. shook

him awake and told him to put on some clothes. He said that

he wasn't leaving, and when asked why told us that he was

suicidal and needed to be taken somewhere. He still refused to

get dressed, and said he needed to "take a shit" before we left.

We agreed to let him do that, but we wouldn't let him close the bath room door so he could lock it and hurt himself. After a couple of minutes of him repeatedly trying to close the door and telling us that he couldn't go with us watching him, we hoisted him off the toilet and again told him to put on some clothes. Again, he refused. Impatient, we handcuffed him while he was still nude. His mother pinned a pink towel around his waist. He said that he was tired of building houses and tired of life. We placed him in the squad car wearing the pink towel, pantyhose, lipstick, and red toenail polish, and took him to Parkland Mental Hospital.

He told us that he had attempted suicide on three previous occasions.

A female bicyclist complained to me about a loud, disgusting man that had rode beside her on a bike

and made lewd sexual comments while drinking alcohol from his water bottle. A week later, I spotted him at the lake on his bicycle and had him stop for me. He told my partner that he could open a water bottle. He must've thought that we would think it to be grape juice, but it was iced wine, and I poured it out.

He received a ticket for alcohol in the park and was never seen again.

A Target store had cash registers on both ends of the store. Many times someone exited on the wrong side, and when they could not find their car called 911 to report that their car had been stolen. They are embarrassed and apologetic when I lead them out the other end and their car magically reappeared in the other parking lot.

Several seconds after driving through an intersection, my partner looked in the rear-view mirror and exclaimed "There's a van rolling over behind us!" "Yeah, right" was my reply as I looked over my shoulder... to see exactly that! We circled back

and found that the woman ran the red light and swerved to

miss an oncoming vehicle and lost control, leading to multiple

rollovers. She was unhurt because of her seatbelt but went to

the hospital for possible whiplash

Before an inebriated male could drive home from a Wal-

Mart, a witness flagged me down about him. He was easy to

find. Staggering around the parking lot with his keys in one

hand checking the door locks of cars that looked like his own, he

was wearing slippers and had a big box of cheerios tucked under

his other arm. He went to Detox.

Normally, the police car that you drove for your shift had

enough gas in the tank because the previous shift officer would

top it off at shift's end. One time apparently neither one of the

officers on the previous two shifts had refueled, and I didn't notice. As I was driving down Central Expressway with a

prisoner on my way to jail, my car started sputtering. I'd driven

cars that hesitated and sputtered some before, but not like this.

I then noticed the illuminated orange low fuel dummy light.

Conveniently, the next exit had a 7-11 on the corner and I

dropped a few dollars of my own money for gas. I did not fill

out a reimbursement form for petty cash; that would've

required an explanation.

Neighbors noticed some late night activity at a house and

notified police, mistakenly thinking it might be a drug house.

Our Deployment (undercover) officers watched the unusual

activity and discovered that suspects were bringing furniture

and other property into the house. The officers obtained a

search warrant to investigate the property. The house was full

of stolen property from literally dozens of unsolved burglaries,

with much of the furniture stacked inside.

This was the only time in my career that I spent much of my day loading and inventorying stolen property brought from the house to a police rented box truck. Some of the burglary victims showed up at the house having seen it on the news, and many of them had gathered to watch. Several spotted some of their property and spoke with an on-site detective, and some spoke with a news media reporter when a news team arrived.

We had a call about two teenage males spray painting graffiti on a business. We saw two colors of spray paint on the wall and set out to locate the delinquents. We spotted them sitting on a bus bench with the same-colored spray paint cans in the grass next to them.   I believe this was the only time that I had ever arrested suspects for Graffiti, which had just become a charge separate from Criminal Mischief.

Things were typically slow at 9pm, the beginning of a shift for a Violent Crime Task Force on a Friday or Saturday night.   I sometimes started my shift by slowly driving through the parking lot of an under 21 club. Human nature being what it is, many people under 21 would sit in their car and drink alcohol before they went into the club, since they couldn't be served. I wrote many Minor in Possession tickets and Consumption of Alcohol by a Minor tickets there.

I stopped an elderly woman for a minor traffic violation and discovered from talking to her that she was lost and trying to get home. She'd been driving the same way home from church for decades, but this day she had to take a detour because of road construction. She had been meandering around for 5 hours looking for a recognizable street. I called another officer to assist me. We were an hour away from her house. I drove her in her car, and followed the other police cruiser. She was very grateful, and we phoned a relative upon entering her home to express our concerns.

I was leaving the County Courts building one morning and had to pass a long line of citizens waiting outside for the slow process of being searched and having their property x-rayed on a conveyor belt. One young man got my attention- -and concern-- when he raised his voice and said "Officer! Remember me?" I thought that could mean trouble, but he actually thanked me for arresting him for theft several months earlier. He said it scared him straight, and he was now a reborn Christian and a law-abiding citizen. We shook hands, and I wished him continued success.

Heading to a disturbance call, I had a vehicle take a fast turn in front of me and drove in two lanes before he settled on one. I drove alongside of him and saw him drinking from a 12 oz. can of Coors light beer. I pulled him over. The suspect's breath smelled of alcohol, he had slurred speech, blood shot eyes and had slow movements. He admitted to having had two beers but

I was unconvinced by his obvious lie and he was arrested for DWI.

His father came to claim the vehicle and it was released to him. When I asked if the father knew why his son was being arrested, he replied "I guess because he's drunk". This comment was placed in the Arrest Report to assist the D.A.'s office with his son's prosecution. At the jail the arrestee told the Intoxilyzer Operator that he had consumed 12 cans of beer, and his BAC (Blood alcohol content) tested at over three times the legal limit.

It was one o'clock in the afternoon.

A female motorist was so thankful of my having given her a verbal warning instead of a citation that she stepped out of her car and tightly hugged me. There were passing motorists, and though I allowed her to do this there was not a reciprocal embrace during the hug. Still, it was a nice gesture.

I was assigned to work the Texas State Fair and a little 5-year-old girl had been missing for over an hour. I sought her during my foot patrol and luckily spotted the little girl run past me from the same direction. I thought that the reason why she was missing for so long was because she was running, and by the time fair goers realized that she was alone, she was well past them. I ran up to her and called down to her "Hi, are you lost?" She looked up at me and immediately recognized me as a police officer and nodded yes. She stopped running, and I told her that she was going to be fine because I would bring her back to her mommy and daddy. She grabbed hold of my fore-finger and we began the long trek back through the crowd to the "Lost Kids Corral" amid many female sighs of "Awww. How cute!"

Most of the lost children at the State Fair are located by police officers or by fair goers and reunited with their parents within twenty minutes. One autistic boy had been missing for two hours. I made a special effort to scan the crowds from my chair lift, which was about twenty feet in the air. He was a labeled a "Critical" Missing Person because of his mental incapacitation. The police would not stop actively looking for him until he was found. I sighted him and quickly lowered my chair lift to intercept him before I lost him in the swarming throngs of people. I succeeded and began the walk to rejoin him with his parents. Unlike the little girl mentioned above, I felt awkward holding hands with this autistic boy; he was twelve-years-old, but nearly as tall as me (6 ft 3).

After leaving the county jail one night having incarcerated a DWI arrest, I was blocks away and found another DWI. Her car was subsequently towed. She had never been arrested before and was nervous and frightened about being in the county jail. She was un-handcuffed and searched by a female jailer. Afterwards, she closely clutched my upper arm against her body the entire time that we waited our turn in the book-in line. I was simultaneously her arresting officer and her protector.

That can be said for all arrestees, but this was very obvious.

Police Officers are almost always honest. Despite what people may see on TV, very few officers in the USA are thieves or corrupt. It just makes for a good TV drama when an officer who is supposed to be trustworthy and honorable is portrayed as a crook who taints and dishonors their badge and oath. In 26 years of police work, I was never offered a bribe in Dallas. From my experience, Police Officers lose their jobs to alcohol more than for any other reason.

One morning after detail (roll call) was over, I was told to drive downtown and retrieve an officer who was waiting up in Internal Affairs and to give him a ride home. I queried why am I giving him a ride home? How did he get there? I was told to just do it and don't ask questions. I arrived to discover that he had arrived publicly intoxicated to Internal Affairs to be investigated for being publicly intoxicated on duty. I felt sorry for him because he was a nice guy who was obviously an

alcoholic.

He was soon terminated.

A man moaned and groaned and asked someone to call 911

for him because he was hurt. His outlandish story was that

while he was walking down the sidewalk during daylight he

didn't notice an open manhole and fell into it. I arrived to see

that the sewer cover was about 75% off the hole and he was

half in it, and half out, and putting on an act like he was

enduring great pain. I saw no scratches, no bruises, but the

ambulance transported him to the hospital per his request. I

suspected he was looking for a City of Dallas payout for alleged

negligence and carelessness from his having fallen into an

obvious hazard that he probably created, and I stated as much

in my Incident Report.

I was walking back to my police cruiser after having gone to municipal (traffic) court. As I began to cross a downtown street, it appeared as if a young male was intentionally shifting his direction to walk toward me. I changed direction slightly and he brushed me as he passed. I watched him over my shoulder and he continued walking, so I assumed this possibly mentally disturbed and homeless (?) male was gone. I walked the 40 yards to return to my cruiser and unlocked it and sat inside. When I looked up, I was surprised to see this same male had turned and followed me and was now directly in front of my push bumper, standing motionless and facing me, blocking my departure from the street curb. What he didn't realize was that the police air horn speaker was attached to that push bumper. After a few seconds of standing directly in front of that loud air horn as I held the switch, he quickly walked away, not having anticipated being blasted by a high decibel speaker.

Early in my career, police had neither mace nor tasers; we had nightsticks (Monadnock PR-24's in Dallas), our pistols, and a shotgun. I made a traffic stop on a driver who was intoxicated. While I gave him sobriety tests his two friends who had been seated in the vehicle decided to step outside. I instructed them to get back in the vehicle, but they said that they wanted to watch and keep an eye on their friend and kept their distance. As I continued talking with the driver, his friends started moving slowly in the darkness to envelop me. It was obvious to me that they were planning to surround me. I backed up to evade the encirclement and placed my hand on the butt of my holstered pistol and sternly said "Back Off!" They stopped, but only briefly. When they began walking again, I again quickly shuffled backwards, this time unsnapping my holster and raising my pistol nearly out of the holster and barked "Get back! Stay back! I'm not going to tell you again!" This time they yielded and obeyed, and when I told them to get back to their vehicle they did so. I arrested the driver for DWI, and we went to the county jail with his car keys in his pocket. I never asked him if he wanted to release his car to his buddies. Their attempts to

overpower me in this tense situation earned them a trip home

by other means.

Some road signs exist as a reaction to a catastrophic event.

At Buckner and Ferguson in Dallas there are some pedestrian

crossing signs. These were placed there after a mother was

crossing the four lanes of traffic with her two young daughters

about 4 and 6 years of age. A responsible mother would have

used both of her hands to hold a hand of each of her daughters.

Instead, she crossed the street with her two little girls holding

hands and trailing just behind her. The mother didn't notice

when one of the daughters stopped in the road to tie her shoe,

and the other daughter who had been holding her hand waited.

That careless mistake became fatal. Traffic was coming their

way and an unfortunate man was distracted briefly in his

vehicle or had a car in front of him swerve out of the way, and

he struck both of the little girls. Though it wasn't his fault, that accident must torment him to this day. Despite the girls having been Care-Flited by helicopter to a hospital, they were both dead within a day. The foolishly reckless and irresponsible mother had caused their deaths, but she had lost two daughters and was never charged. A lifelong burden of guilt is a heavy load to carry.

I was in a loss prevention office watching a thief on camera use a trashcan to shield his actions from any cameras. He was using a box cutter knife to remove price tags and plastic security sensor tags from merchandise all the while looking around for witnesses and believing that he was beyond the view of the cameras. We followed him remotely on camera but lost him briefly. When he was seen again he was passing by the loss prevention office heading for the double exit doors. I rushed out the office door and saw the shoplifter entering the double door lobby just steps away from being outside. I ran and maneuvered around a couple of incoming shoppers, then made use of the suspect's sweatshirt hoodie. I grabbed it and yanked

back, asking "Where are you going?" then yanked harder,

pulling him off balance and onto the floor, then handcuffed him.

He never had a chance to run or wield his box cutter to resist.

He nervously cried and stuttered in the loss prevention office

before he went to jail, claiming that he normally didn't do that

sort of thing. I think he meant that he normally didn't get

caught.

One night I responded to a Shots Fired call coming from near

a creek area. When the other officer and I pulled up together to

the location by an apartment complex, we viewed several

teenagers standing several yards in front of a large green

building generator. I advised the other officer that one of the

suspects had placed a pistol atop the generator as we pulled up;

he hadn't noticed. As I calmly approached the group I told them

that someone had reported shots being fired from the creek

area and asked if they had heard or seen anything to allay their

fears that we possibly suspected them. When they spoke and
started to lie to us, I was close enough that I jumped and
grabbed the suspect and took him to the ground and cuffed
him. I then confiscated the pistol that was behind this group.
The suspect had hoped that I wouldn't notice his sly and covert
weapon placement in the darkness.

He went to Juvenile for UCW (Unlawful Carry Weapon). We
had no witnesses for a charge of Unlawful Discharge of a
Weapon within City Limits.

A friend had gone to his birthplace in Tanzania Africa. He
bought me a souvenir t-shirt "How to Speak Swahili" with about
15 expressions on it. I only memorized the first two of "Hello"
and "How are you", but that came in handy on a few traffic
stops. The African-born motorists were flabbergasted when a
half-world away a uniformed white officer greeted them in
Swahili with "Jambo! Habari Gani?"

Those Dallas Police sure are smart.

It was night and a 20-year-old didn't know that the set of headlights behind him approaching the red light that he was waiting on to change belonged to a police car. When the light went green, he sped away and I stopped him doing 90mph in a 45. He said he was upset because his laptop computer had been stolen. He shed a few quiet tears when he received a speeding ticket. I told him that in my 22 years of being an officer I had never seen anyone drive that fast on this street, and he said he understood.

He was a good respectful kid, and I felt a little sorry for him.

An officer viewed a motorist who had stopped her car and was now personally pulling a dead dog to the center median. It had just been hit by another driver who had kept going. He called for cover and I saw from my laptop map screen that I was nearby. The dog was well groomed and had a collar with an owner tag. The compassionate motorist called the owner, then left and returned with her husband and an old shower curtain. The dog's owner had arrived before their return and was sobbing. We were all safely on a wide median, so I didn't need to rush her grief by hurrying her along. When she was ready, I told her of the shower curtain to transport her beloved dog back home. I carried the still warm medium-size dog by the legs with his tongue hanging out and placed it on the shower curtain with care, then folded over the excess plastic to encapsulate the family pet. We placed the animal in the owner's trunk, and I gave her the phone number to Animal Services in case she didn't want to bury it herself.

A passing park patron called 911 to report that a man was sitting at a picnic table and seemed to be calm, but he had a gun pointed at his head. We rushed over to the location code 3, then cautiously walked over to the man so that we could ascertain what he was doing. It became apparent that he wasn't pointing a gun at his head, but rather had a "Dickery Doo" in his mouth and was playing the musical instrument. He was amused by the incorrect assumption that someone had made and started phoning friends.

A man went into a busy bicycle shop and test rode a racing bike in a small parking lot across the street. He commented that he was going back to Colorado in one month and wanted to buy a good bike before he left. He was watched by an employee and said he liked the bicycle but that it needed some adjustments. The man rode back near the store and started a conversation with a regular customer. The employee assumed that he had a sale so he allowed himself to be distracted by some other customers. The man on the $3700 bicycle was never seen again.

A man entered an auto parts store and lingered too long, bringing suspicion upon him from the employees. They observed him place some merchandise inside his shirt, and shortly afterward try to leave. He triggered the theft sensor at the exit. An employee asked him to come back to the office. The man was insistent that he didn't take anything, stepped back through the detector, and triggered it again. "Sir, step back into the office and we'll talk about this." "I didn't steal nothing." This time he rushed out and didn't return. I arrived after the 911 call and asked for a description of the suspect. I was told "He left his wallet right there." Sure enough, there was a wallet atop one side of the theft sensor device. Like at an airport, he emptied his pocket to prove he didn't have anything (employees knew better) and put his wallet up there, forgetting to take it when he fled. I walked over to the wallet, pulled out his photo ID and asked the employee "Is this the man that was in your store and stole your merchandise?". "That's him officer!" amidst co-worker laughter. The suspect's wallet went to the property room as evidence of his presence and crime.

A 65-year-old woman was taking her 7-year-old Poodle for a walk. She was across the street from her house when two Rottweiler's belonging to a neighbor jumped over the fence and charged toward her dog. The female Rottweiler stopped, but the male Rottweiler dog never slowed down and attacked her leashed Poodle. The Poodle owner tried to steer her dog away, but the snarling Rottweiler had a firm hold on her dog's throat and she couldn't. An ex-Navy SEAL neighbor overheard the commotion and looked out his window, then quickly rushed over with a short piece of wood and started pummeling the aggressive bloodlust dog. The dog quickly released his hold on the Poodle's face and throat and ran off, but it was too late. The Poodle was dead.

The attacking Rottweiler was confiscated by Animal Control for quarantine, and the owner was cited by them for having an insufficiently high fence to properly contain his dogs.

We received a tip from an informant that a young man had stolen a car and was mostly storing it in his dad's garage to hide it. Peering through the overhead garage door window, we saw the license plate and confirmed that it had been stolen via a computer check. We knocked on the front door and spoke with the father who had no idea the car was stolen; he was just doing his son a favor. He had no misgivings and allowed us to remove the vehicle to tow and return it to the true owner.

I worked for a police department in a city that had over a million residents, but there were still some sparsely populated areas in Dallas like around parts of Lake Ray Hubbard. This only happened once in my career, but we drove upon two cows on a rural road. My partner had put them out to pasture before (in the literal sense) and knew where the hole was in the fence. Between his activating his siren and air horn as he drove toward them slowly and my walking slowly toward them from the other side waving my arms, I directed them back through the gaping

fence hole. We filled and blocked it with dead branches and
contacted the owner.

I was just leaving municipal court downtown when I made a
traffic stop on a motorist two blocks from the courthouse for
running a red light. I wrote her a ticket for one of a possible
three citations, but still she complained. She had also just left
the traffic courthouse about a previous ticket and now she was
getting another one.

A woman ran a red light, and I made a U-turn to pull her
over. By the time I caught up with her, she had driven to the
rear parking lot of a city building. I cited her and also arrested
her for DWLS (Driving While License Suspended). When I
returned from the county jail, I entered her workplace back at
the scene of the arrest and spoke to the manager. He had only
been there a few weeks and was hired from another state to
amend some internal problems. He was concerned and

shocked when I told him that I had just arrested one of his employees who had been driving with a suspended driver license for six months.

She was a city of Dallas DART (public) bus driver.

White Rock Lake is the most popular and crowded recreational spot in Dallas. During nice weather, hundreds of bicyclists use the trail and roads daily. There are accidents every year involving bicyclists and motorists, so in an effort to minimize this number, there are signs at some stop signs that inform bicyclists by state law they must obey the rules of the road. This included stopping at signal lights and stop signs, and the racing cyclists know if they ignore the law it is at their own peril, both from a possible citation and a possible accident with a car, bicyclist, jogger, etc.

I was riding a police bicycle when I observed a bicyclist look to his right (possibly seeing me) and pedal through a stop sign at the bottom of a short hill. I tried to pedal my heavier mountain bike hard to catch up to the racing bicyclist, but the best I could do was get within 25 yards and shout "You just ran that stop sign. You need to stop!" He ignored me and didn't stop, and I quickly lost him. But the lake bike trail/streets used by bicyclists is a full circle. I just rode in the other direction for a few miles, then dismounted my bike and waited for him.

Sure enough he appeared, and I stopped him on the road. He wasn't very happy about getting a ticket.

I was riding with another officer at night when we heard a loud crash and drove over to investigate. Someone had struck and toppled a light pole on the center median. We arrived just seconds after it happened and the call had not yet made it to the dispatcher. As we pulled up and exited the police cruiser, we saw a male running through the darkness, and quickly found out from a witness that he was fleeing this accident. We rushed toward where we last saw him using our flashlights to illuminate our way through the pitch-black darkness, but we didn't see him. Then we heard a loud metallic "klaaaang!" A little further we could see that the fleeing motorist had ran at full speed into a long metal pole that was laid across the entrance of a closed business to keep vehicles out. The pole was parallel to the sidewalk and one foot over the pavement. The suspect had slammed his shinbone into the pole and he had flown several feet and was now rolling around in pain on the ground. We called him an ambulance before we transported him to jail for DWI and FLID (fleeing the scene of an accident by Failing to Leave ID).

His leg probably hurt even more after he sobered up.

I stopped a vehicle that I had seen smoking for about a ½ mile, with a large plume of smoke trailing behind it. It had smelled like burning brakes as I drove through the smoke. I spoke to the old man and his wife and they were surprised when I showed them that their emergency brake was engaged. Who knew how far they had driven like that?

I shined my spotlight at a couple in a PU truck that was parked on a scenic overlook at the lake, then walked over and shined my flashlight into the vehicle. "Just making sure that ya'll are not doing anything you're not supposed to be doing out here." Without missing a beat, the girl replied, "Not with him!" and we both smiled and laughed at his expense. Realizing then that he wasn't getting any action that night, he drove off a few minutes after I broke contact.

I arrived at a condominium complex fire when a resident informed me that he heard a loud explosion and thought maybe a plane had crashed into a building. That was not the case. There was only one condominium on fire, with massive amounts of dark gray smoke billowing out the windows. Gradually the flames were extinguished by the fire department, and just some wisps of smoke remained. A fireman thought that somehow a refrigerator had exploded.

A woman new on the scene told me that she knew for a fact

that the female owner put her three dogs in metal cages under

the stairs when she was away. I relayed this to a fireman, and

within minutes they brought out all three dogs, dead in their

crates from smoke inhalation. Firemen will try to save pets

when possible, but they were hidden from view and they hadn't

seen them. It was probably already too late for the dogs

anyway when the firefighters first appeared on scene. A

relative of the condo owner showed up and said she would

watch over the dogs until the owner arrived. The owner was an

hour away and neither I nor the firemen wanted to be there to

see the anguished, grief-stricken dog owner. Losing one dog is

hard enough, but to lose all three at once?

While patrolling with my window down, I detected the odor

of marijuana coming from a car with three girls. They had been

smoking outside until they saw me and retreated into their car.

I circled and popped on my emergency lights. I found no

marijuana but did write a ticket to the owner for possession of drug paraphernalia, a pink rhinoceros smoking pipe.

I stopped a motorist for driving 40 in a 20 mph school zone. He said he never saw the flashing yellow light. At this time, we needed to record info for traffic stops, so I took his DL back to the police car. Minutes later I returned it and gave him a verbal warning. Before I could drive away, the man got out of his car and walked back to me and asked "Did you keep that driver's license thing?" "No sir" I replied to the 87-year-old, "It's in your hand". He looked in his hand, waved to me, then got back in his car and left. It's tough to get old.

I pulled over a vehicle for two reasons: The man had a headlight out, and he was driving the wrong way on a short one-way within the park. The motorist stepped out with my permission. After he turned off and then turned on his headlights, somehow (maybe a loose connection) both headlights were now functioning. He told me that his headlights were fine. I told him that one wasn't working minutes ago. "Yes, it was" he retorted. I said, "No, it wasn't." He again said that his headlights were both on. I informed him that one was not and took his DL back to the car to write him a ticket for driving the wrong way on a one-way.

   When I returned, he coarsely told me "I know what this is all about. I was argumentative. I just spent the last few minutes telling my kid why you're such a prick!" Reminding him to take care of the ticket within 21 days, I simply said "Have a good night".

   Driving up to a grocery store on a shoplifting call, I parked my police cruiser in plain sight in the fire lane directly in front of the store. It was daylight. While I was upstairs processing the thief, one of the managers were viewing the shopping floor from the upstairs window and exclaimed "We got another one!" I was incredulous how this could happen with my car so plainly visible, and I'd like to think that the thief was already in the store when I parked there. Because of the dollar amounts involved, one thief was transported to jail, while the other received a theft citation.

During my shift I accompanied another officer to jail and left my squad car on the center median of a street full of speeders. Later in the day I spoke to a friend of mine when I was working a side job. I told the arrest story and mentioned where I parked my car. He laughed and said "That was you? I was running late for work and speeding when I saw that cop car. I thought he had me, so I slowed way down hoping he wouldn't stop me. Then I drove past and looked and there ain't nobody in there!"

Mission accomplished.

I headed to a call involving a naked man shooting at a woman in the street. Upon arrival, I learned that the suspect had awakened to a woman screaming for help. The man looked out of his window and saw a snarling angry Rottweiler dog chasing a woman, who climbed up a tree to escape the carnivorous canine. The man ran outside in his underwear with his .38 caliber pistol. When he reached the tree, he fired off a warning shot into the ground near the dog, and the loud gunshot caused it to retreat quickly.

The dog owner was located, and he was warned to repair his fence so his dog couldn't escape from his yard before someone got hurt and/or he was ticketed for dog-at-large by Animal Control.

Near the end of our shift one evening, I told my rookie that we would check a few license plates of cars in an apartment complex parking lot, that maybe we would get lucky and find a stolen vehicle and get a little overtime. After running just a few license plates, we did locate a stolen vehicle. He was baffled and so was I; sometimes police work involves simple luck.

Having made an arrest at White Rock Lake for U.U.M.V. (Unauthorized Use of a Motor Vehicle), I was walking my handcuffed arrestee to my police cruiser when a young man interjected. He was a tourist from Denmark and asked in accented English why the man was arrested. After I told him that he had been driving a stolen car, he asked if he could take our picture. I halted and said sure he could. The happy tourist snapped a photo of us and thanked me.

I can't be certain, but I'm pretty sure that I was the only one smiling.

A woman was stopped for running a red light. I wrote her a ticket and returned to her vehicle and she was crying. I reminded her that it was just a ticket and not the end of the world. She told me that I didn't understand. She was having a

bad day. She had just found out that she had breast cancer.

"I'm sorry" I said. I let her regain her composure, and when she

turned to face me, I ripped up the ticket.

A Sam's Club employee surprised me when I learned that she

was caught up in a fraud scam. Having worked there as an

officer for many years, I knew her. She had falsified many

phone applications, and the phones for these fictitious people

actually went to two young men who paid her a fixed amount of

money for each phone that she delivered. This girl was a friend

of mine, had two kids, and was now responsible for about

$20,000.00 of phone thefts. I gave the investigating detective

her phone number, so he could attempt to convince her to roll

over on the other two suspects for a deal to minimize her jail

time. I hope that she cooperated.

A woman got upset after her boyfriend returned home after an all-nighter, having drank plenty of alcohol and having spent too much of their money. They began to argue, and the man was injured.

I arrived to see blood all over his clothes, the wall, the carpet, and two blood-soaked rags that he had used to control his bleeding. The woman had cut him on the connective tissue of his left hand between his thumb and forefinger using a small Exacto knife with a blade shorter than two inches. I asked what had happened. The man stated "She cut me! I can't believe she cut me!" The woman that I arrested for Aggravated Assault was unapologetic and simply said "He was harassing me so I cut him!"

Two brothers aged 8 and 10 were missing for several hours. The parents waited several hours before they reported them missing, just assuming that they were somewhere in the neighborhood and were not too worried about them.

The boys took public buses and a train. On the train platform, a Transit Officer questioned the boys about who accompanied them. The boys had done this before and were streetwise and pointed to a nearby woman, which satisfied the officer. She was a stranger. The boys also had some money that they had used to buy food, drinks, and snacks. Because of their young age, the call was a "Critical Missing" meaning that officers would continue generating leads and make efforts citywide to locate them until they were found.

Other Transit Officers found them when their agency was notified by ours of the missing boys, and I retrieved them to meet up with Dallas Officers from South Dallas who would transfer them home. While I waited for these officers at the designated rendezvous spot, the brothers were laughing, giggling, and carrying on about their exciting day, not at all concerned. I knew from their happiness that they were sure to disappear again in the future for another bold and brash adventure, and that again more police resources would be expended to diligently locate them.

An intelligent woman received a phone call from a man who used the name of her 20-year-old nephew. He sounded nervous and worried and said that he was arrested in North Carolina while on vacation with some friends, and they all had too much to drink. It sounded like her nephew's voice so when he asked that she please not tell his mom and requested that she help him out with his bond money, she readily agreed. He thanked her and said that he would pay her back, and put his alleged attorney on the phone. The attorney introduced himself and was very informative and professional and told her the bond was $1000. He advised her that the quickest and most efficient way to get this done was to go to a store and purchase a Green Dot Card for that amount and even suggested some stores that she could use. She went to buy one, scratched off the code, and gave it to him over the phone in under one hour.

Afterwards, she began to doubt the veracity of the story and went online to find that the phone number belonged to an attorney's office in Quebec, Canada. The person that she had been talking to would not answer her calls. The aunt called her nephew and learned that he was at home and hadn't gone anywhere. She was duped out of $1000 because she had a generous, sympathetic heart, but the whole scheme could have been thwarted had she phoned her nephew in the first place.

There was a city sponsored festival on the City Hall Plaza, and a number of officers--me included--were assigned to make sure things went smoothly. Suddenly, we saw many of the attendees rushing toward us, followed by a horde of people coming our way. I asked aloud why everyone was running, and one of the fearful evacuees said that someone had a gun, while another said that someone was firing a gun. This showed me how quickly disinformation can spread panic. While everyone dispersed from the center of the crowd, I and other officers rushed to the center with drawn weapons to encounter the alleged gunman. I didn't think any shots had been fired because none of the officers had heard anything, but we believed that somebody probably had seen a pistol from careless or intentional brandishing by a suspect and began the stampede when they announced it to others.

In any case, no gunman was found and ten minutes later everything was back to normal.

While returning from a different county jail after delivering an arrestee to them, we heard an alarm sounding from a closed library. Though it wasn't Dallas, I decided to check the building to be sure it was secure. It was still daylight and the Rockwall Police Officers had not yet arrived. I pulled into the parking lot as a man in a car was about to pull out of the parking lot. We both looked at each other and slowed down. We rolled down our windows and he said that he didn't know what had happened; he had just dropped his books in the book return and the alarm had gone off. I told him jokingly that there was

no reason for that to happen unless there was a bomb in the

books, meaning that level of a vibration would trigger the alarm.

I could tell by the look on his face that he was not amused by

that remark, and I thought that some people are just humorless.

My partner ran his license plate as the man drove off, and

then laughed. The registration returned to a Middle Eastern

male. I had said my remark innocently enough, but this male

would probably forever think that I was stereotyping him as a

potential terrorist because of his origin. I had unintentionally

given the police department an undeserved black eye from my

seemingly innocuous comment.

A woman arrived to a friend's house one night to pick her up

and see a movie. As she turned onto the street, she caught a

glimpse from her passing headlights of a man standing in a dark

recess of her friend's front house wall. He was wearing a gray

sweatshirt with a hoodie and only a few feet from the front

door. The woman was not about to step out of her car and drove a few houses down the road to be sure she was safe, then called her friend to alert her. She in turn relayed the info to her husband and he stepped outside in his bare feet. He looked to the left and saw the startled suspect, who ran back along the house behind the bushes. The barefoot husband ran out to the sidewalk to look down the street and saw the suspect running under a streetlight in the distance.

The husband and wife had a shed burglarized one month earlier and as a reaction had a CCTV Security Camera system recently installed. We watched the suspect on video but would never know what his intentions were that night. Peeping Tom? Robbery? Burglary?

Only one time in 26 years did I volunteer be a "Santa Cop" to deliver wrapped toys to needy children. The premise is wonderful, having uniformed police officers deliver gifts to some of the community poor whose names were submitted during the year by officers who came into contact with them in the span of their duties. It's good public relations for the police department when people see officers happy and smiling. I submitted the names of several people that I had arrested or to whom I had written tickets when I saw or learned that they had young children who didn't have much. Why not spread a little holiday cheer?

The kids may have been happy and smiling, but for the four-hours that I delivered gifts the parents were always ungrateful and melancholy. I think they were so used to getting generous handouts that they expected assistance throughout the year and the whole experience was blasé for them. In one home, I could tell that the relatives who happened to be visiting were so embarrassed by the parents' lack of gratitude that they felt compelled to thank and praise us for our delivery.

I never volunteered to do it again, although I still think it is a good positive police public relations program.

I stopped a 32-year-old woman at 12:30 a.m. for not having her headlights illuminated. She was intoxicated, and I conducted several sobriety tests. While saying the alphabet she stopped at G, then skipped to L, stopped again at P and said "I'm sorry". She failed the tests and was arrested for DWI. Her husband stopped by being driven to the location by a friend. All had come from a bar. The husband offered to drive her car but he too had too much to drink and I told him to get back in his friend's vehicle. The woman had said she had "two or three beers", but her BAC was later .16 on the breathalyzer test. She had met her husband at the bar to celebrate their 10th wedding anniversary but had decided to leave after they got into an argument.

A suspect who had been drinking alcohol kicked open the front door of a duplex, then walked inside, scaring the teenaged brother and sister that were watching TV. The drunken man wearing black gloves only walked a few steps when he was confronted by the father. The drunk put the father in a headlock and announced "It's time to die!" The teenage son reacted and walked toward the drunk, who grabbed a picture frame from the wall and threw it at the son but missed. The father broke free and the drunken man ran back to the front door to escape. The father grabbed a tire iron and tossed it at the man but missed and it only damaged his own wall. The family of three all ran out the door to pursue the ambling, drunken suspect. An undercover/deployment officer spotted the four of them running on the parking lot of a nearby apartment complex and handcuffed the drunken suspect. Oddly, the intruder and the family members did not know each other. The suspect was arrested for "Burglary with intent to commit a Felony" because of his forced entry being followed by his comment to the father of "It's time to die!"

The burglar was actually very nice to us and had a great sense of humor. This was his first felony and I really believed that it was completely alcohol induced and he would have no recollection of events when he sobered up. I did him a favor.

On his Felony arraignment form, I documented his cooperation,

good attitude, and lack of felonies on his criminal record for the

magistrate.

Sunday mornings are usually very slow for police officers too.

You generally had time to get a leisurely cup of coffee from a 7-

Eleven, which was my intention. However, when I cleared for

service, I received a call about a woman who had waited almost

an hour for the police at a Total service station. She waved at

me from a payphone as I entered the parking lot.

Nine hours earlier at 11:30 p.m., a man put his hand

over her throat and told her that he could kill her if he really

wanted. My female complainant had made the mistake of

allowing a homeless female friend to move into her apartment

seven months earlier, and two months later this "friend" had

invited her boyfriend to live with them. The man was now a

roommate, which made the minor assault family violence. The

complainant had just walked around and slept outside the last night, though in very pleasant weather, and the soles of her bare feet were blackened from dirt. I received the names and birthdays of the female and male, hoping that they both had warrants and that I would then solve the unwanted roommate's situation for her by taking them to jail. Only the male had warrants however, but they were serious ones, both "Sexual Assault with a Child." One child was 15, one 16 at the time of the criminal offense, while he was currently 29. It was still before 9 a.m. and this 5'3", 140 lb. suspect was still presumed to be in the apartment. I asked for another officer for cover, and received a FTO (Field Training Officer) and his rookie. We went to the apartment and I told the complainant to see if the door was open while we hid around a corner. It was locked, so she knocked. As soon as the door began to open, we rushed forward to also enter the apartment. I looked to my left when I stepped inside and observed the suspect sit up in bed upon seeing us. I rushed over to grab one arm while the rookie grabbed the other, and the suspect was quickly subdued and handcuffed. The warrants were confirmed good (valid). I told him what the warrants were for and asked if he knew the ages of the girls at the time he had sex with them. He did and showed no contrition. He was meek and mild-mannered, and said that he was afraid to go to the Dallas County Jail because he had heard that it was bad there. At this time there were no chairs to sit down and watch TV in the holdover area at the jail like there is now; everyone had to sit or stand on the cold concrete floor behind a yellow line until your name was called.

A man was arrested for DWI. On the way to jail he often stuck his tongue out to lick his lips and twitched, indicating probable drug use too. He told me that he made a mistake and that he was a new man and it wouldn't happen again. Next he told me that he needed a drink. After a brief pause he realized what he said and said he didn't need a drink, he needed a chance. Freudian slip.

Wearing a ballistic (bulletproof) vest was optional for most of my career. As a bicycle officer the last 7 years of my career I generally almost always did not wear it, especially during our hot Texas summers. When I worked as a Patrol Officer answering 911 calls the first 18 years of my career, I always wore my ballistic vest-- with one exception. Murphy's Law played a role that day, and I never shirked wearing my vest again while I responded to 911 calls.

I was getting ready to go to work, but my vest cover that had been in the wash was not yet dry. I decided that I could go one day without wearing my vest, that most calls for service that I answered were non-life threatening. I left my bulletproof vest at home.

During my shift I ran code 3 to a shooting call, and a man that had been shot in an apartment complex parking lot was taken away by ambulance. A minute later, the crowd that had gathered began to part up the middle, and a man who had stepped into the crowd was suddenly standing alone with everyone looking at him from the crowd now on both sides of him. Breaking the silence, a woman said "Officer, he's the man that shot him!". I un-holstered and pointed my pistol at the Aggravated Assault suspect and ordered him to put his hands up, which he had already started to do on his own. I directed him to get on the ground and he complied. I cuffed him and searched him, but he had no pistol or any other weapon. He wanted to surrender and not be a fugitive from justice for his crime.

A 19-year-old girl was at a Western Union late one night and filled out some paperwork at the counter. Soon she had an unpleasant conversation with someone on a specialized telephone, and slammed down the receiver so hard that she broke it and walked out in disgust. The very next person who tried to use the phone told the clerk that the phone was not working. The clerk found the paperwork for the angry girl, and I made a Reckless Damage report listing the damage at the replacement cost of $800. I'm sure the girl was upset because someone didn't send her money, and now she had increased her debt and had even less to her name.

A woman waved her arms to get the attention of a passing police officer. She told him that the man who raped her last night "just got on that bus" as she pointed to it. The officer got a suspect description, and requested the dispatcher send some cover officers. We followed the bus, and when enough officers were present we waited for the bus to stop. Another officer and I blocked the front of the bus, while a third officer stopped behind. We boarded quickly but could not immediately ascertain the location of the suspect until we saw the identifiable brown trench coat that he had been wearing on the floor beside him. The suspect was snatched up, handcuffed, and led off the bus. The other passengers were dumbfounded and aghast at the whole ordeal.

Once off the bus, the suspect asked and answered his own question.

"What's this about? Is this about a woman last night? A black girl?"

His Res Gestae statement was put into his arrest report.

I went to a signal 27, which for us is a dead person call. The fire department had called, pronouncing the complainant dead about 15 minutes earlier, but they were not there upon my arrival. At the apartment building, the nephew was waiting outside to walk me to the apartment. We went inside, and I saw a teenage girl, two older women, and a man in a wheelchair all in the living room, sitting and watching TV with their backs to me. I started to walk to the back bedroom, and as I did I asked "Where is he? In the back bedroom?" expecting him to be in there. The nephew responded. "No, he's right here in the wheelchair." No one was talking or crying, just watching TV quietly with the dead man beside them.

The 63-year-old had died of lung cancer and had been in a wheelchair for weakness and bad knees for decades.

Many years ago, when someone had mental issues that could put themselves and others at risk because they couldn't focus on reality, we would handcuff and transport them to a psychiatric hospital by using the politically incorrect term "Lunacy Warrant." It was just documentation to justify their need for a psychiatric evaluation and to prescribe meds.

One such complainant was found in a grocery store parking lot talking to himself and to others who were not within earshot. When asked what he was doing he said he was waiting for the solar eclipse (he was 8 days too late). The man said some deranged things. He was perfection which was given to him for all that he had done, even though he had a shrill voice like Satan (?). He couldn't die because of a touch from God's hand. He spoke all languages, and English with a Japanese accent (He was white). He lived and died and then lived again.

He would be made whole again and then new again. God told

him to hurry up and get ready because today was his day.

It was indeed his day…. to go to the Parkland Hospital Psych

ward.

On a hot summer day, I received a call regarding people that

were skinny-dipping at the spillway of White Rock Lake. I

doubted the accuracy of the call because there hadn't been any

rain in a while and I couldn't imagine there being any water in

the spillway. Soon I saw that the report was true. The four

people were sitting in a shallow bowl-shaped pool of water at

one side of the spillway. Two men wore blue jeans while a man

and his girlfriend were naked. We ordered them to dress, and

soon found the common denominator; all were intoxicated.

Three went to Detox by Paddy Wagon, and I drove the

remaining man to his home because he had AIDS and he didn't

want his friends to know. He still received a citation for his

drunkenness.

Being HIV positive was an automatic trip to see the county jail

nurse, which was further and more time consuming. I was

happy to oblige him and release him to the custody and welfare

of a neighbor.

An 18-year-old tried to cash a check that didn't belong to

him. His signed endorsement of the check took him from no

criminal record to having committed a felony. He was

handcuffed by the gun wielding owners of the check cashing

business who rushed around the counter and out the door into

the customer lobby area to take him into custody. He was

seated on the floor when we arrived (this business alone

probably provided the Northeast Patrol Division with ¾ of our

arrests for Forgery when they were open).

The arrestee stated that he had been working for a married

man for four months when the man made some sexual

advances toward him. This 18-year-old employee thought he would get back at him by cashing a large un-cashed check that he had seen in a desk drawer that had been there at least since he started working there. The kid was shocked when I showed him the print on the check showing it was only valid for 90 days, and we were well beyond that.

I learned later that the boss dropped the charge against the 18-year-old in exchange for his silence on their romantic encounter.

At 11a.m., a woman walked to me with a sense of urgency and flagged me down. I could see that her car behind her suspiciously had two flat left tires. Two flat tires on the same side is a tell tale indicator the driver has bounced off the curb or median too many times. Sure enough, she was intoxicated and had been driving her car drunk, but there were no witnesses. She should've flagged police down when she was sober. She went to jail for public Intoxication, possession of marijuana, and

possession of drug paraphernalia (crack pipe).

I went to a construction site where I was told by the foreman

that he had found an unauthorized man stealing on his

worksite. The suspect dressed like a workman and was even

wearing a hardhat. He confronted the man and called the

police, but the thief just ran away. I advised him that if it

happened again that any citizen--including him and his crew—

could make a citizen's arrest for any felony, theft, or breach of

the peace. If need be, I told him they could even hold the man

down for police if it came to that.

A few days later there was another call for the police at the

same location, and I took the call. The same suspect was seen

putting a drill into his car. This time when I arrived I could see

that the foreman had taken my advice because I saw about a

dozen of his workmen standing in a circle, surrounding the same

thief who had tried to steal some power tools again. Most of the workmen held hammers, or a board, or a pipe in their hand,

which successfully intimidated the suspect into not attempting

to escape. I had the Foreman give the suspect a criminal

trespass warning, and took the suspect to jail for his day's

earlier theft offense and some warrants.

The arrestee wanted me to know that they had called him

some bad names and insulted him while they waited for me.

Several days after 9/11/2001, someone began mailing the

deadly white powder of Anthrax to some Congressmen and

important people, and several people died. For months

afterwards, we would get the occasional call from some people

who believed whenever they saw a white powder in a letter or

package that it had to be Anthrax, and that someone was trying

to kill them. We were told to take the calls seriously. I had

several calls regarding this, including a woman who found an

envelope out by her trash can in her alley that had a

"suspicious" white powder in it. The real Anthrax was always sent to a prominent person to make a statement that no one

was safe, but even a few average people (by definition most of

us are) started believing that they could be targeted.

All of the letters or packages that were tainted by the alleged

Anthrax were placed in a footlocker outside of the main

property room. All of that "evidence" later tested negative for

Anthrax. Other than wearing rubber gloves to handle these

potentially lethal Anthrax envelopes, we all had no protection

and would have easily inhaled the Anthrax toxin spores and died

had any Anthrax been authentic.

On February 1, 2003 the Space Shuttle Columbia

disintegrated upon re-entry into Earth's atmosphere, killing all

seven astronauts aboard. NASA said the debris field would

stretch from Louisiana into east Texas. Though it was a long

shot, Dallas Police were told it was possible but not likely that

some debris would land in our city. The debris was being

collected so that engineers could reconstruct the Columbia from the junk to try and determine the cause of the failure.

I had one call for an item in a Popeye Fried Chicken parking lot, but other than possibly recognizing a heat tile, or something large, who knew what Space Shuttle debris would look like?

The odds of being stopped by a police officer on any given day are extremely slim. However, once I stopped a motorist for an expired registration, but gave him a warning. He had a ticket written to him by an officer in another city just 15 minutes earlier. In a metropolis with millions of people, that was astronomically unlucky to be stopped by police twice in a quarter hour.

I spent a half shift watching an Aggravated Robbery prisoner at Parkland Hospital. When another police agency spotted a wanted DPD suspect, they had pulled him over. To escape, the inebriated suspect made the impulsive decision to run and jump over the guard rail on a bridge at night. He was five stories over the road below. He lived, but with a pelvis broken in four places.

Things are not always as they seem, or as they are reported by citizens. Sometimes they are worse, sometimes it's nothing at all. I heard a car alarm go off in a parking lot at my Sam's Club job, and stepped outside to investigate. I saw two employees staring in the direction of the alarm, where a car had lights flashing. One employee said, "There is someone breaking into that car!" I bolted over, and the car was now backing up with the lights flashing, and the alarm still sounding. I soon discovered that the driver was a senior citizen and I tapped on the window. She stopped and opened the door to apologize, saying it was a rental and she didn't know how to silence it. I turned her car key in the door lock and that did the trick.

I will speculate and say that while most police officers in the USA would love to kick in some doors, most in fact have not. Circumstances allowed me to kick in several doors during my career. Once, a woman had returned home to find that she couldn't enter her apartment because it seemed to her that someone had thrown the deadbolt from the inside. I knew from experience that in all likelihood, the deadbolt was simply frictionless and partially slid into the lock from the vibration when she closed the door behind her when she left. She was adamant that someone must be inside and gave us permission to kick in her door. I had a rookie who had never kicked in a door before, and now was his chance. I showed him where to place his kick. He hesitated, and I realized that although he was twenty years younger than me, he probably couldn't get his leg up that high. It was starting to rain and we didn't need to get any wetter, so I delivered the one kick door opener.

As I had suspected, no one was inside.

A woman wandered into a small hospital near White Rock

Lake and began talking to nurses in the Emergency Room. After

having her vitals checked and hydrating her on that hot day, the

staff felt comfortable that she was no longer a heat casualty and

wanted to release her. They felt that considering her

conversation that perhaps a police officer should take her

home. They called to ask if an officer might be nearby to stop at

the hospital. I volunteered and was informed by a nurse that

she wasn't sure about the woman's mental condition and if

what she said was true. She claimed to be the stepmother of

Officer Aubrey Hawkins whose name was still recognized by

many even 12 years after he was killed on Christmas Eve 2000

by seven escaped Texas prisoners. As a city of Irving police

officer, Aubrey Hawkins diligently and quickly responded to a

Hold up Alarm at a sporting goods store and drove to the rear

where he was ambushed and shot to death by the fugitives.

Police drive victims and witnesses home on a regular basis,

and I drove this woman home. She told me that she had raised

Aubrey since he was 7 years old, and after losing him she also had to cope with a daughter that committed suicide. She had trouble with depression but was on the road to recovery and lived in an assisted living home.

At the ride's end, she thanked me and shook my hand, adding that I was a very nice officer. She missed talking with Aubrey and other police officers and I could see that all these years later, just saying that had brought tears to her eyes. I thanked her and wished her well after I walked her to her door.

I was inside a 7Eleven store one hot August day enjoying a cold drink. A customer walked in and I informed the man that his zipper was open. He made his purchase and left. The very next customer to walk in also received the same comment from me. Public servant at your service.

Several officers and I were at a house that had just been burglarized. The neighbor saw the group of suspects and reported it, but we missed them by ten minutes. I drove off to search for them and quickly spotted the five burglary suspects walking down a wide grassy strip across a six-lane road. They had just turned the corner and I'm sure were heading to the Dallas Area Rapid Transit (DART) train. The 3 males and 2 females were all laughing and smiling until they spotted me, then their joy became quiet timidity as they averted their eyes away from me. I broadcasted my location and a few other officers were soon assisting me as we quickly took all into custody. Right place, right time.

It was just one day earlier when I had found five other burglary suspects as a secretary back at the police substation later commented.

A woman was vacuuming her living room rug when her boyfriend told her to not do that so early. The man heard a ruffling noise and went to investigate and found the woman dumping his marijuana on the carpet intending to vacuum it. He became angry and the woman told him that all he cared about was smoking weed. She told him he slept too much and needed to wake up and pulled the curtains off the bedroom window to brighten the room. The man gave the woman a hard shove and she fell against a wall and sustained a cut elbow and cut lip from the assault. I arrived at the location and asked the man for his ID. He said aloud to his girlfriend "Where's my wallet at?" The woman replied "It's under the couch pillow where you keep your marijuana." I moved the pillow and found a small baggie of marijuana. I cuffed him for his family violence assault, then looked in his wallet that was under the same pillow and found an even larger weed baggie.

I covered an officer that had requested another officer at her accident site. I volunteered since I was just down the street. I was disgusted when I arrived and saw her on a sidewalk waiting for an ambulance to come and assist a couple of people in one of the cars. I spoke to them, a seat belted grandfather and teenaged grandson and they assured me that they were unhurt as far as they could tell. I told them to tuck their heads and hold onto the seatbelt as they lowered themselves; they were hanging upside down in their overturned vehicle.

My Sergeant and I were riding our bicycles at White Lake Rock Lake when we heard a very loud boom from hundreds of yards away. It sounded like a large chunk of concrete being dropped into a metal dump truck. Seconds later, we heard two sets of two gunshots. We looked at each other and agreed that they were gunshots, and I broadcasted "shots fired" to the dispatcher. We hustled to the area and heard two accelerating vehicles and saw one of them drive away. We asked the remaining driver if she had heard the gunshots. She corrected us and said the noises were actually from her husband's 30-year-old truck which we had just seen departing on our arrival.

She had been following him to a mechanic shop in case he didn't make it there. The backfires from this truck were amplified across the lake surface and were the loudest we had ever heard.

A mentally slow 19-year-old girl became separated from her mother at the lake and called her mom on her cell phone to say she was lost. The mom called 911 to report that her daughter was lost at the 9 mile diameter lake, but somehow the mom provided her own description to the 911 clerk, so we were mistakenly looking for a woman in a pink top and black biker pants. In spite of it being a hot 95 degrees at the lake with few people, we found three women fitting that description. The last one found was the mother who clarified the clothing description of her daughter. I finally located the lost girl when I got out of my car and walked over a hill and descended down to the lake. There, I found the girl sitting on a bench facing the nearby shoreline. Poor girl. It hadn't occurred to her to be visible to her mom or anyone else who would be on the street or a parking lot looking for her. She was only visible from my having walked over this hill.

I turned down a residential street and seconds later I saw there was a car coming toward me from the middle of the street. I could see that the driver's head was down and she was somehow distracted. Expecting an imminent crash because I had nowhere to go to avoid her, I stopped and felt for my air horn switch at the same time, which I never did find. Luckily, she looked up and the 16-year-old girl was able to stop two feet before a head-on collision. She had no driver license and had decided to go for a short drive alone for the practice. The drive was much shorter than she expected, as she never even left her block.

I sent her home with her first traffic ticket for "No DL". She probably never tried that again.

A man had been arrested in a gravel parking lot after me and a few others arrived to assist the original officer who expected the suspect to possibly fight to avoid being arrested. After he was arrested, he saw his opportunity to try to make a run for it as several officers were seemingly distracted in conversation. He only made it about ten yards before he slipped on the stones and slid headfirst halfway under a police cruiser. We pulled him out and informed the genius that he would now also be charged with Felony Escape since he was a handcuffed prisoner.

He had done this right in front of his girlfriend who was on the scene. We let them say their tearful farewell. Afterwards, with the attractive woman still crying, I told her that her boyfriend was a loser. I said she should have some dignity and self-respect and find a better boyfriend. She could do better and deserved better, and I asked why she was still with him despite all of the crimes he had committed in his past. Love truly is blind because her only response was that she loved him.

We had a call one Sunday morning regarding a homeless male that was sleeping in the Post Office. It was my idea that we should roust him from his slumber by barking at him loudly like a couple of Drill Instructors. As expected, he awoke with a startle and gathered his things and scurried out the door without saying a word with us shouting at him. He benefitted at least from not receiving a citation for sleeping in public, or going to the city detention center for a violation of the city's anti-solicitation ordinance, a warrant which many of the homeless had. Still, after we had initially laughed, we agreed that it wasn't very polite and a rude way to wake up.

Given the previous entry, it would be appropriate to mention a positive contact that I had with some homeless men. It was about 10 p.m. one night and I was leaving the parking lot of a Sam's Club after I had finished working there as police security to make some extra money. I had seen a few homeless just west of the store lately and had anticipated that they would be there again. I saw them and stopped my car. Concerned charitable people had apparently done this before, as three homeless men began walking toward my car to receive a presumed donation of some sort. They didn't expect a uniformed police officer to step out, and they walked away hurriedly. I told them to wait, that this wasn't some kind of trap. It was winter and I had brought about a dozen pair of socks. Many had a small hole in them somewhere, but as any police officer who has taken homeless people to a Detox facility or jail can tell you, when the socks of homeless people are removed and shaken out for contraband, it is quite a stinky experience. All of those socks were fresh and clean, and I was sure these men would put them to good use.

At night a man driving a stolen car bailed out and ran into an apartment complex, and I ran through a small field to get to that same complex from a different direction. I only went several yards when I fell, having tripped over a large chunk of concrete that was in the field, and slammed my right knee on another concrete chunk when I fell. I could have been impaled on some of the exposed rebar that was embedded in the concrete from my fall, so it could have been worse. I was in excruciating pain and thought I had just given myself a lifelong knee problem. I now slowly walked and felt my way through the concrete chunked field in the darkness. Someone had done some illegal dumping and I suffered from it. I emerged from the field limping as officers were roaming around with their flashlight beams hoping to find the suspect. After some minutes passed, the belief was that he must not be there, and must've kept running. Soon the officers congregated in a parking lot, and only me and a security guard remained, still searching for the elusive burglar. I shined my light beam in the small interior fenced patio of an apartment, and as I was scanning I saw the crouched suspect trying to go unnoticed. He was partially hidden by an object. I was careful not to let the illumination linger on him or he would bolt once again, and I was in no condition to follow from my temporary injury. I continued scanning with the beam and said aloud so the suspect could hear "I wonder where he went? How did he just disappear like that?" I then turned off my light and motioned for the security guard to come to me, and whispered "Get the other officers." He ran to the parking lot, and they all returned. I pointed to the low fence enclosure and quietly said, "He's in there." He was taken into custody within fifteen seconds.

All laws, even the lesser-known city ordinances, should be enforced periodically otherwise they never should have been enacted in the first place. After handling a disturbance call, I noticed that a neighbor a few houses away had foot high grass in the front yard. This normally wouldn't have bothered me, but I had just become a proud first-time homeowner and was adamant about doing something about this homeowner who obviously (in my mind at the time) took zero pride in home ownership and was a blot on the neighborhood. I wrote the woman a "High Grass" city ordinance ticket, the only time that I cited someone for that violation in my whole career.

A woman and her boyfriend had just finished reading a book about edible mushrooms and were anxious to find some real ones in the woods. Some flooded areas had receded recently, and the maximum surge waterline mark could be seen on the trees and the forest floor. They spotted what appeared to be a large white mushroom growing by itself in the distance. Soon they saw that it wasn't a mushroom, but a human skull.

I responded to their call and located the tattered remains of a tent. It was obvious that many months had passed since the probable homeless person's death. No other bones were found. The medical examiner bagged and tagged the skull, then went to his downtown Dallas office.

As I arrived at my dinner break location, I noticed something shift by my black windshield wipers outside the glass. It was a black stream light flashlight that the M.E. had left behind when he was processing the skull using my hood as a desk. I phoned

him after dinner and made a trip to his office. It was about 9

p.m. but a slow night and he was kind enough to give me a

supervised tour. I was surprised that a short hallway that

connected rooms had the worst stench of death. The other

rooms that I was shown were cold to minimize the rate of

decomposition, and therefore the odor. All of the bodies were

zipped up in heavy rubber body bags.

I saw one corner with a few body bags on gurneys. This

would likely be where our skull would end up. When all tests to

determine the identity of an unknown person are inconclusive,

and all leads exhausted, these unfortunate souls are labeled as

"Joe Doe" or "Jane Doe". Eventually they are buried as paupers

with the simplest of headstones. They are obviously missing

persons, but missed by whom?

How few would be at their cemetery interment?

--"At birth we bring nothing with us; at death we take nothing

away"—Chinese proverb.

Standing in the book-in line at Lew Sterrett County Jail, I noticed a large-lettered tattoo covering the forearm of the prisoner in front of me. I commented "You do know that your tattoo is misspelled?"

"Yeah, my sister did it for free. I should've paid someone to do it" was his reply. The tattoo was supposed to be "SOLDIER", but instead spelled "SOLIDER".

Another arrestee had a tattoo of "Forgive me Father for all of My Sins" across his chest.

Citizens regularly call for police when they see something or someone that appears suspicious. We received a call to investigate two parked, occupied vehicles that were facing each other from opposite sides of the street. A neighbor had noticed that they had been there for hours and it was suspicious. As we cautiously approached one of the drivers, I could see that he was watching our approach from his driver side mirror and was attentive to his surroundings. When we arrived at the vehicle, he was ready for us. He flipped open his wallet to reveal a badge and an I.D. card. Secret Service. They had been assigned the duty of protecting one of the then 41st President's George H.W. Bush granddaughters, a daughter of the future 43rd President George W. Bush. She was attending a slumber party.

I left thinking that theirs was an important, but boring career.

A bicyclist flagged me down at White Rock Lake and led me to a distraught dog owner. The owner had been walking her dog in the park without a leash and the terrier dashed over and into a muddy hole near a creek, probably created by a nutria which is a large aquatic rodent. The owner was trying to coax her dog to come out, but we could just hear his muffled barks from inside the black mud hole. I called for animal control and told the dog owner this would have been prevented had she had her dog on a leash in the first place. Her two daughters echoed that sentiment. We still didn't know if her dog was injured or stuck and couldn't exit the hole, or if the terrier just didn't want to escape. The brave owner decided to wade the shallow creek and bank that was near the original hole, put her arm in a muddy cavity on the creek bank that was near the original hole, thinking she could possibly reach in and grab her dog by the collar and pull him out. I'd be afraid of getting bit by her dog, or a swamp creature. All that happened was that she pulled out a muddied arm.

Animal control arrived, and I started to help him dig a larger entrance at the hole, but the mud was wet and heavy. After jabbing a pitch fork into the ground at the entrance to loosen up some of the dirt, shaking the ground in the process, the dog was frightened enough by the trembling earth that he suddenly emerged and stood about two feet from it. The dog saw daylight and several people. I had a sensation that he might retreat to the solitude of his muddy den when he paused. I jabbed the pitch fork down behind him to block the hole and defeat his retreat, which is exactly what happened when he turned to try to re-enter the hole. The woman took her dog home after I told her the dog needed to be leashed the next time she took it for a walk. She smiled and said she learned a lesson.

A naked man was reportedly sitting on the front steps of his apartment. I mistakenly assumed that he would be gone by the time officers arrived. I soon saw that I was wrong; he was still sitting nude on the stairwell. I tried to talk to him, but he was unresponsive, looking dazed, stunned, confused, disoriented, with slurred speech and dilated pupils. I tried to get him to stand up but he was tense and stiff. I briefly thought that he was under the influence of cocaine or crack, but I didn't see any needle marks on his body, nor did I see any drug paraphernalia. I saw the other officer had now arrived, so I stepped into the man's apartment to see if anyone else was inside as the door was standing wide open. Like his mind at the moment, no one was home. I heard running water and went into the bathroom to turn off the cold water that had been pouring into the bathtub. A maintenance man stated that the man had sat outside for almost an hour. I found some clothes in his bedroom and we helped him get dressed. Going through his wallet, we found a Medic Alert ID card indicating that our complainant was an epileptic. We called an ambulance to examine him for his epileptic episode, and they transported him to the hospital for observation and as a precaution.

Officers responded to a Burglary-in-progress call and got into a foot chase with the burglar after they spotted him exit a window of the burglarized home. I arrived and saw the officers arresting the burglar in a small field and provided spotlight illumination to help their night vision. The suspect was placed in my car. He said that he just moved in with his sister, didn't have any friends, and was just outside walking around. He admitted that he only had the idea to break into the house because he happened to see the residents leave.

Unsure if there were other burglars in the house and thinking that shots reported fired in the area near the time of the burglary might be related, the decision was made to surround the home and broadcast a message to any remaining burglars: "This is the Dallas Police Department. The house is surrounded, come out with your hands up." This P.A. System message was articulated about 20 times, as well as a few "We are sending in our dogs!" (a ploy, my idea). Eventually, a ballistic shield was used to enter through the front door, with about 5 officers following. No one else was in the house on this slow cold night, and about 15 of the 18 police cars left the location. The sole burglar went to jail.

A man rented a Home Depot Truck and brought it back to his apartment complex. He had two friends get in for the trip, then placed the truck in gear. It surged so fast backwards and slammed into a Mitsubishi Mirage so hard that the collision broke the window, crushed the door and pushed it out of its parking space.

He had only traveled 10 yards into his road trip and hadn't even left the parking lot.

Driving through an apartment complex, I went around a corner and there were two young males in a car heading in the opposite direction. I saw the expression on their faces as we passed each other, and they exuded fear and worry. I struggled to maneuver to make a U-turn with cars parked on both sides of me. When I did and went back around the corner of the building to where they had been, I saw the vehicle. It was now unoccupied with both front doors opened, but there was no sign of anyone. Sure enough, the car had been stolen. Both suspects got away, but at least I had made them pedestrians and recovered a stolen car.

Many years ago, when another officer and I were always interested in maximum enforcement activity, we stopped cars on the freeway that had been waiting to finally drive past our accident scene. Traffic would be very slow because of multiple lane closures due to an accident. While we waited for the wrecker trucks to arrive, and just as motorists were relieved to finally almost be driving the speed limit again, we would wave them over for their expired registration or inspection stickers and write them a citation.

The government isn't always inefficient.

Just before I transferred to White Rock Lake to be a bicycle officer, I trained my very last rookie. I always strived to expose these young fresh police academy graduates to as many diverse calls as possible for them to gain experience and to force them to think and learn. The first few days on the streets is a rookie officer's observation period, where he could just sit back and acclimate himself to being in a police cruiser and calm his nerves while the trainer does the police work.

When queried, my rookie decided to hit the ground running, so we did. In his first seven work days out of the police academy, we had 19 arrests. These included Possession of Cocaine, Possession of Marijuana, felony DWI, Aggravated Robbery, Evading Detention, a couple of arrests for ticket warrants from other cities, and a bunch of arrests for Public Intoxication. We also answered about 30 calls, wrote seven tickets including possession of drug paraphernalia, and recovered three stolen cars and a pistol.

One of the Public Intoxication arrests happened as we were finishing up a traffic stop and heard a flurry of activity with some yelling and shouting from a Taco Bell a ½ block away. We drove over to investigate and observed several college girls in a vehicle using the drive thru, a few of them were hooting and hollering while standing and using the open sun roof. I engaged them in conversation and they were reluctant to admit that they had been drinking alcohol because most or all were probably underage. One girl volunteered that she wasn't drunk and that we could test her if we so wanted. Her friends were skittish and intuitively realized that such an action would be a big mistake. They quickly tried to negate their friend's willingness to prove her sobriety, but to no avail. I raised my voice and said "Sure, come on down!" The girl ignored her friends' pleas and dipped down out of the sunroof, out of the car, and walked over to us. She was happy and smiling, until I did a simple HGN test on her eyes and she failed. She was arrested for Public Intoxication. Her tears reflected her regrettable decision.

She and her friends probably still reference that story from time to time.

Most arrested people are cooperative with the police. Many will tell you that they know that you are just doing your job. Most arrestees are not violent and don't want to resist arrest, and don't want to hurt the officer who happens to arrest them. When affecting an arrest, many officers will ask the arrestee if he has any knives or drugs or needles on them, or sometimes to be amusing if they have any machine guns, grenades, or bazookas. There was one time after I had handcuffed a male that I asked whether he had any knives, drugs, or needles on him, but while searching him with rubber gloves I neglected to wait for him to respond. I stabbed my right middle finger with a hypodermic needle prick. He had an upside down syringe in his pant pocket without a protective cap on the needle. I pulled out my hand and squeezed the finger to force blood drops to the ground. It was a shallow puncture, but the needle had still penetrated my skin. It was just Hepatitis that I had to worry about, or so I thought. My heart sank when he told me that he was HIV positive and had AIDS. I summoned an ambulance and a supervisor.

After a test, I had to wait an insufferably long two weeks to discover that I was HIV negative.

We met some paramedics at a home for the mentally and physically disabled as they were leaving the building. They had just left the upper floor apartment of a deceased tenant who was found dead on his couch. They informed us that the stench was bad, as the man had been decomposing for over four days. Although it was winter, a recent warm spell caused him to turn off his heat, and we were grateful for that. The odor could've been worse, but it was still overwhelming. I held my nose shut and was still on the verge of gagging. The man had died with little dignity, sitting on his couch wearing only a t-shirt, naked from the waist down. Gravity had forced a large amount of blood from this 350 lb. complainant to gorge and swell his lower extremities. Gravity had also caused an interior detachment of muscle and fat to drop from a vertical area at his chin to his chest as he decomposed. A pistol was found on the bed of another room, but he had no roommates and the front door had been locked from the inside. There was no sign of foul play.

He had been in poor health, having a dozen prescriptions for several different maladies.

   The Medical Examiner body snatchers (my term) used a reinforced gurney to strap in the obese decedent. Movement of a body always creates a worse odor, and I stood in the stairwell trying to breathe fresh air from the open windows. One of the employees had given me a can of deodorizer/room freshening spray, and I kept my forefinger pressed down firmly on the spray nozzle mainly for my benefit as they passed me on the way down to their vehicle.

   At 8:30 p.m. one night as I came around a turn at White Rock Lake, I saw a vehicle veer off a street and start driving uphill. Initially, I had thought he had turned up a parking lot entrance ramp but now realized that he was driving on the bicycle trail. I drove over and popped on my emergency light bar behind him about fifty yards up the trail. The 18-year-old driver said that he was taking his girlfriend on a date. I commented "I'm guessing that you don't have a driver's license?" He replied, "No Sir."

When asked, he said the car belonged to his grandpa and that

his grandpa knew that he had the car and that he had no driver

license. He explained "My Grandpa lets me drive his car

because he knows that I'm a good driver." I couldn't resist, and

while grinning said "Well, you're not impressing anyone

tonight." His girlfriend couldn't stifle a big smile. He received a

No DL ticket and I explained how he made his mistake and lead

him back to the road.

An early afternoon arrest had forced me to skip my lunch.

Driving to the gas pumps to refuel prior to getting off work, a

motorist braked hard in front of me to make a turn without

signaling, forcing me to slow suddenly. Already on overtime,

and irritable from an empty belly, I decided that I'd just get a

few more minutes of overtime and make a quick traffic stop. A

check of the motorist DL determined that he was driving on a

suspended driver license.

When it came to finances, Dallas was and is like most cities I suppose. There are times when the city was flush with cash, and other times when the city was tight-fisted and very reluctant to pay employees overtime. This time fell in the latter category. I radioed for a cover element(unit) to come and transport my prisoner to the county jail. An officer was sent who was at the start of his shift. I explained to him what I had, and at the end he surprised me by telling me that he didn't like the idea. I reminded him that I would be waiting on the wrecker and doing the report. All he had to do was transport my prisoner and sign the warrant. He bluntly told me that it was starting to rain, and he didn't like to take prisoners to jail in the rain. He went back to his car and drove off. I was flabbergasted and riled by his answer and his laziness. The wrecker arrived in short order, and I finished the wrecker sheet and hauled my prisoner back to the police station and found another officer to transport my signal 30 (prisoner) without any fuss. I complained to the original officer's sergeant. He was unconcerned, and I knew from his cavalier attitude that nothing would be said or done about it.

Unfortunately in Government jobs, the cream doesn't always rise to the top. There are energetic, industrious officers that get promoted, but so do some lazy officers. What matters is how well they score on the Civil Service exam. That unhelpful slug of an officer eventually became a Lieutenant.

The dispatcher reported that a black Ford Explorer was blocking the right lane of a street. I had just passed by there and had seen that the owner had moved his truck to a side street for safety, so I informed the dispatcher to disregard the officer who had been en route to the call. Minutes later, there was another call about the black Ford Explorer. I took the call and circled back and spoke to the young man who had been driving the truck. I found out that he had called 911 both times. The first time he had called to get an officer to change his flat tire, and the second time was to get a ride home from an officer. The audacity. He said he knew how to replace his flat tire but thought an officer could help. I told him then he needed to fix his own flat tire, and that the police are not his personal taxi service. Police do occasionally change flat tires for women or the elderly and give people a ride home when they were involved in an accident, or they are a victim or witness to a crime, but don't call emergency 911 for a tire change or to get a ride home. Make other arrangements. 911 clerks usually do an outstanding job of screening calls, but sometimes unnecessary calls slip through.

I think most police officers and many mental health professionals would agree that nowadays as a society we are over-medicating people to treat them for depression and other afflictions rather than counseling them and treating the root cause of their unnatural mental state. Police have too many calls regarding those with mental health issues, many more than decades ago.

A woman called because she was concerned about some strange actions by her husband. We arrived on the scene to find her husband standing on the front sidewalk, staring up into the sky, watching the light from a cloudy sunrise. The woman came out the front door to greet us and was crying. "He went to California for four days and came back crazy!" she told us. Still looking skyward, the shirtless and shoeless husband began speaking to us. "Look at this beautiful sunrise, look at the beautiful day that the Lord has made." During the two weeks that he was home he had been verbally abusive with his wife, and she feared for his and her safety saying she didn't know him anymore. He had told her that over in California he had seen God, and that he was Jesus Christ the son of God. She was all for people getting a little religion, but his having the God complex was too much.

Prior to our departure to the Parkland Hospital Psychiatric Ward, the wife nervously allowed her handcuffed husband to kiss her goodbye on her cheek and shoulder as he said "Bless

You. I love you." He had been institutionalized in one about a dozen years before their marriage.

The entire distance to the hospital was marked by the man tilting his head back atop the rear seat to look through the window at the sun behind the clouds as he happily engaged us in conversation. He didn't stop looking up until he went indoors.

The Fire Department called for police after responding to a call and finding a large man dead in his bedroom. They had a strong gas-powered blower flan that was being used in a vain attempt to aerate the house, as the obese man had been dead for at least a week. His body had turned light gray in color and had what appeared to be a hair-like red fungus growth on parts of his body.

I doubted if the surviving relatives would hear the whole truth from the Medical Examiners Report. No reason to embarrass the deceased. The polite and diplomatic truth was that the man

died of a heart attack while sitting on his couch watching a

movie. The harsh reality but complete truth was that the

seated naked man had died of a heart attack while

masturbating and watching a pornographic movie.

At Sam's Club, an older couple had entered through one set

of exit doors and waited for a flurry of customers to pass them

by so as to enter the store through the interior exit door. I

could see that they may have to wait longer than they expected

because the store was busy. I reminded them

"This is the exit door. The entrance is on the other side."

"It's 102, do we have to go around?"

"Everybody else does, what makes you so different?" He gave

me a nasty look, then walked outside and went around to the

entrance.

When he finished shopping, he came to the exit door where I was still standing and said

"I didn't appreciate that smart ass remark. You could have been more sympathetic and said that you understand that its hot outside but that you'd appreciate it if we went around."

He was right. I think that we as police officers can be testy and verbally spar with good people at times, and this was one of my examples. I didn't apologize, but I didn't want to add any fuel to the fire either, so I just said "Be that as it may." I knew better than to argue over something this petty. He was leaving, so why would I prolong contact by responding and possibly incite a real confrontation? Still, it was difficult to bite my tongue when he walked past me and said "Make sure it doesn't happen again!", as he strutted like a proud peacock to impress his wife.

It was mid-March, and the lake water was probably about 55 degrees. As I was patrolling the lake, several people saw me and silently waved and crossed their arms in the international distress signal fashion. I stopped and found out that a young black dog was swimming about ten yards from the shore, and I actually saw and heard him panting and yelping like he was afraid and exhausted. It seemed like he was in danger of drowning, but he didn't come to shore. The owner was very anxious. His dog swam at the dog park but then crossed a narrow cove of the lake and was now 200 yards from shore, and still going. A bystander jumped into the water when the crying dog was a little closer to the lakeshore then snatched it and brought it ashore. Rather than stay, the dog was disoriented and wanted to return and hurried back to the water's edge. Now the owner acted and jumped into the water to grab his dog and kept it on shore for its safety.

I used my P.A. system to call across the narrow bay to have the dog owner's friend bring the car around, which he did. We concluded that the dog must have been stressed from hypothermia, having been in the cold lake water too long and was confused.

I responded to a burglary call, or rather an alleged burglary. A 70-year-old woman met me and said that she had been gone several hours the previous day. When she returned, she discovered a bag of groceries by the bed and didn't know who put them there and that they should be returned to the owner. Illogically, she had prepared an itemized list of the groceries and concluded that nothing had been stolen. Mysteriously, though no one else had a key, she believed that an unknown person had somehow entered her locked apartment and left the groceries in an effort to drive her crazy (mission accomplished). She said that all of her doors and windows (which all had burglary bars) had been locked. A couple of boys rode by on bicycles, and she exclaimed while looking out the window "There goes one of them now!"

She had to think twice about her birthday when I took her information for a Social Services Referral. Someone would look in on her and determine what city mental health services could

be available to help her.

I had arrested a male for a theft from Home Depot. He had

no identification, so he was fingerprinted and it was determined

that he had many alias names. The arrestee knew about the

Parole Violation that he had out of Alabama, which became an

add-on charge to his theft when his extradition was approved

by that state. However, the AP (Arrested Person) told me that

he was surprised that he didn't have a warrant from DPS (Texas

Department of Public Safety, or our "State Troopers"). I had a

conversation with him and he didn't suspect that I would alert

DPS by faxing over an Incident Report to help them pinpoint his

felony Evading Detention in which he fled and escaped from

them. He stated to me that he had pulled over during a traffic

stop on I-20 in the Big Springs, Texas area around 3 A.M. with

three other males in the car. Knowing that he had the Alabama

Parole Violation and a marijuana pipe inside the driver door where he sat, he quickly ran and was not found. I felt confident

that with my description of the car, the event, the arrestee, and

date, time, and place, that he did not elude justice after I faxed

over my report for their scrutiny.

We went to a 911 hang up call and upon knocking at the door

we heard two children's voices in unison say "Who is it?"

"Dallas Police, open the door." Now both children began to cry

and one of them said that their Mom told them not to open the

door for anyone. After a little encouragement, I convinced

them that we were there to help them and asked them to

please open the door. Upon entry, we saw an untidy apartment

and no adults at the scene. Their mother returned to the

apartment a short time later and asked us what was wrong. The

two kids were still crying and afraid. I told her that a 911 call

came from her apartment. With a scowl, the mother turned to

her daughter and told her that she was going to get her ass

kicked, and that she had better shut her little mouth and stop crying. The mother stepped outside to speak with the other officer, during which time the crying and shaking little girl said to me through tears "She's going to whoop me!"

A routine check of the arrestee showed that the mother had a county warrant and unpaid Dallas PD traffic ticket warrants. The mother was arrested for those warrants, and for two counts of Endangering a Child, both felonies. The children, aged 5 and 7, were left with a Great Uncle. It was determined from a call to the arrestee's employer that she had been at work for 4 hours and worked 5 days a week.

The children told me that they never had a babysitter.

I made two consecutive traffic stops and wrote a couple of tickets. The first went to a motorist with the last name of Weaver, the very next traffic stop to one with the last name of Cleaver.

The comments on a signal 40 (Other) was that a female was inside a Bank trying to cash a stolen check. I arrived and was told by the Branch Manager that a man sitting outside on a railing had initially entered the bank with the female suspect, who was still in the lobby. I directed the male to go inside and join his female friend. The usual "What's the problem officer?" was voiced by the male accomplice. The other officer arrived. I handcuffed the male without knowing the extent of his involvement before he had time to think about things and possibly run (the cuffs could always be removed if he was not involved). The female suspect now presumed she was next to be handcuffed, so she rose from her chair with her purse and walked to the employee break room door which lead to the restroom. I asked her "Where are you going?"

"I need to use the restroom."

 "Get back here! You're not going anywhere. Handcuff her!" I directed the other officer who was nearer, and he did.

The female suspect had 6 same-sized egg-shaped balls of marijuana in her TRANSPARENT CLEAR PLASTIC PURSE. The female arrestee had gone to the bank to cash a $2500.00 check with the lower left "memo" notation being "Gift". The teller was a little suspicious of the large dollar amount of the alleged "Gift", and told her younger sister/suspect that she could not cash the check for her. Instead of leaving the bank, she simply and senselessly slid over to an adjacent teller. This teller had overheard the first teller refuse to cash the check, and so obtained evidence to prosecute for a check forgery. She told the suspect that she needed to endorse the check, provide a thumbprint, as well as a driver license and a social security card. This teller and the teller who was the sister of the suspect walked to the rear to alert their boss to the probability of a forgery, as the suspect's thumbprint came back on the computer as an "ID Alert". The owner of the check could not be contacted to confirm the forgery, so the offense report was done but no arrest was made. Eventual contact with the check owner was imminent, so the suspect would go to jail for her crime after the Forgery warrant would be issued by the assigned detective at that time. This day though, she just went to jail for possession of marijuana, and her male friend was released after a subject check showed that he had no warrants.

Comedian and former Tonight Show host Jay Leno once called the station and asked to speak to me. I was not available, so instead I received a message. The female officer who answered the phone told me that it sounded just like him, and I assured her that it really was him.

My dad had died and left three beautiful, pristine cars: a 1967 Red GTO with 30,000 miles, original owner, and a 1973 and 1974 Trans Am SS models. I had the idea to write Jay Leno knowing of his love for collecting great cars, and mentioned that I would love to have him go with me on a police ride-along the next time he was in town. He told the other officer to tell me that he had so many cars that if he bought more and spent more time with them his wife would be asking for a divorce.

While driving at White Rock Lake at night, I noticed that a vehicle some distance behind me had its bright lights on, and gradually got closer. Being annoyed by the high beam glare, I pulled over and then pulled back onto the road behind the vehicle after it passed me, and did a traffic stop. The young girl didn't know that it was illegal nor how bothersome it could be to other drivers in front of her. I told her that I wasn't going to write her a ticket, but that I was going to follow her for the two more blocks at the lake to give her a dose of her own medicine. She good- naturedly smiled and said "How Rude!" I gave it twenty seconds before I turned off my bright lights so that she could see the intensity of the mirror glare. I think she learned a lesson.

Responding to a disturbance call, we were told by the man who answered the door that there had been a disturbance but the woman who had caused it had just left. For her safety, we told him that we needed to check his apartment to make sure

that no one was there. He invited us inside and we soon saw

that he lived alone. Unfortunately for him, we also saw the

three-foot-tall potted marijuana plant growing on his balcony.

He was arrested for M/A possession, despite his lame

explanation that he was taking care of it for a friend who was on

vacation.

This took some coordinated maneuvering and use of finger

pointing and the cruiser P.A. system, but I stopped two cars at

once for running a red light. I thought I had made an error and

had somehow written the first drivers first name on the second

motorist's ticket, until I realized that both men had a first name

of "Tracey", an uncommon man's name.

A man was moving into his new apartment in a high-crime

complex. It was pouring rain when a vehicle pulled into a

parking space nearby. The new tenant was carrying some

belongings when he was confronted by two suspects, one from the front and the other at his side. One suspect pointed a pistol at his head and demanded "Give me your fuckin' wallet!" "What?" "Give me your fuckin' wallet!" he repeated. The man slowly reached for his wallet, then opened it to show the suspects that he had no cash, not even a dollar. A suspect asked "What do you got in the car?" "Not much, mostly kids' stuff, some toys, and some clothes." One suspect said "Today's your lucky day", and they got back in their car and sped away.

A new software system that Dallas adopted for its police patrol officers was implemented about a year after we had received training for it, making our training virtually useless. It was obvious to us that the software developer did not retain any police officer as a consultant. A pull-down property menu had all kinds of unique items that no one had ever reported as stolen (like "Gold bars"), but neglected to include "wallet", "purse", or "handbag" as an option which therefore had to be listed under "miscellaneous". When it came to denominations of money choices in a report, it listed $1000, a bill that no one has ever seen, but did not mention a $2 bill as a choice. If an error message appeared, it read "NOT PREOPERLY INITIALIZED" on the screen. How could any misspelled word make it to the final version of a software product?

I stopped a vehicle that had a registration and inspection sticker that had been expired for several months. I caught the driver in a lie when she told me that she just picked it up from the repair shop that day. She also had no insurance, and warrants for her arrest from Dallas PD and a suburb. I wrote her three tickets but overlooked her traffic ticket warrants. Her vehicle was towed as per department policy for no insurance. Her car was a mess inside, and she had probably forgotten about a metal marijuana pipe that she had at the bottom of her center console. She received another ticket for possession of drug paraphernalia. To show her contempt and disdain for me, three times she declined an offer of a ride from me, forcing her two girls under 10 years old to walk nearly two miles with her to get home.

In the mid-afternoon, I responded to a shots fired call. I went to the rear of the approximate apartment where the shots had been heard and found a bent and damaged screen door on an unlocked patio door. I notified other officers and entered with weapon drawn and noticed a large amount of spilled marijuana on a living room coffee table. After unlocking the front door for two other officers to enter, we searched the entire apartment and it was empty. A brick of marijuana was found in an open bag inside the balcony storage closet. I found a .25 caliber shell casing on the kitchen floor and a bullet hole in a vertical blind.

A couple of witnesses had noticed two suspicious men standing around the parking lot near the apartment, and a couple of other men sitting in their vehicle near the apartment before the gunshots were fired. After the gunshots, the two men that had been sitting in the vehicle were seen loading two large garbage bags that we now believed to contain bricks of marijuana.

The brick of marijuana, a calculator, a small scale, rolling papers, a metal drug paraphernalia kit, and 9 small potted marijuana plants were placed in the property room as evidence against the at-large tenant, and Narcotics was notified.

Another marijuana dealer or perhaps a customer had decided to temporarily put this dealer out-of-business.

A pet micro pig was apparently abandoned by its owner at White Rock Lake and had been seen several times by park patrons out in the open, even eating grapes from someone's hand. We thought that the intelligent pig was too domesticated and simply bored. It was last seen running across a six-lane boulevard a few times like it was playing a game before it was struck and killed by a car.

The lake isn't always just the usual crowd, and has some unique characters. Once I saw a man in regular clothes running down the bike trail carrying a banjo. Another time, I observed a shirtless and pant less male, running across park grass wearing gym shoes, a large blue baby bonnet, a giant diaper, and sucking on a large pacifier. He had to have been a radio personality who lost a bet. The bike trail was also where I observed the same two young cowboys with hats, jeans, boots, and belt buckles walking and holding hands on many occasions.

Approaching a vehicle after a traffic stop, I saw a skinny, haggard-looking female driver wearing lipstick who also had a deep voice and an unshaven scrubby face. I looked at the driver license and saw that I was talking to a "Gloria", and the DL picture was that of a blonde woman with a narrow face. That somewhat dispelled my doubts about the gender until I keyed the DL into the computer and saw that I was indeed talking to a male. You can fool yourself by changing your name, but unless you present gender surgery re-assignment paperwork to the state, the government wouldn't go along with it just because you self-identified as a woman. I returned to the driver with some tickets and asked why he hadn't amended his vehicle oversights. He started to cough and told me "I'm not going to lie to you sir. I have full-blown AIDS." This was the early 1990's, a time when there was much less knowledge and much more paranoia about AIDS, so I kept my distance and tried not to inhale much as he signed the tickets.

A man lived near the bike trail on the north side of White Rock Lake. He disliked the busy bike trail, so to avoid it he would sometimes escape all trail users by going for a quiet stroll in the woods, exploring in solitude. He didn't let high weeds and tall tubular shoots stop him. In the woods about 100 yards away from the bike trail, he saw something and took a closer look. He wasn't the only person there. He returned home and called the police, then went back to the forest edge where he directed me to follow him after my arrival. He showed me the other person, or rather what was left of his skeletal remains. I first saw a dried muddy sock still attached to the left foot bone, still connected to the tibia-fibula bones. A few feet away lay the two whitened thigh bones, near the pelvic bone. The rib cage was no longer intact and had collapsed into a messy rib pile. I found a collarbone nearby. A dozen feet away were the partly buried, still intact hand bones, and that many feet in the other direction was the skull. This was an overflow area of the creek, evidenced by assorted piles of twigs and sticks, and by a child riding toy that had been caught in the tree branches three feet above the ground (but the remains were of an adult). It appeared that an intact body had become entangled in branches during flooding, and then over time with the ebb and flow of water it broke up against the trees and forest debris.

I finished the report and my shift before the Medical Examiner departed, and read in the newspaper the following day that when the tattered clothing was removed with the remains that a wallet with ID was found too.

    Patrolling White Rock Lake, I saw a man, his wife, and child having a picnic on a blanket under a shade tree, all wearing swimsuits. There was a multi-colored beach ball with them. I stopped to just remind them that there was no swimming allowed at the lake, and they said they were aware of it.

    I made an arrest not long after I broke contact with them. While I was at the county jail processing my arrestee, the beach ball blew into the water. The man waded out to get it but the water was suddenly over his head and he couldn't swim. He drowned. Police had responded, and his body was recovered and taken to the M.E. Office.

    Hours later when I returned from the jail I drove by the spot where I had seen the family. No one was there, but the beach ball was spookily still adrift along the shoreline, bobbing up and down on the waves.

The criminal offense of "Gambling Promotion" is typically enforced by the Vice Unit, and very seldom by patrol officers. Most states have lotteries, Nevada and many cities around the USA and many Indian tribes have legalized gambling. Those who operate as gambling promoters outside the law, such as "bookies", must occasionally be arrested so that others take notice.

I assisted our Vice Unit with an arrest of a bookie who was operating out of his house. He had a "Gambling Promotion" warrant for his arrest, and was brought to jail on his biggest betting day of the year; it was Super Bowl Sunday just before the game began. I doubted that he could ever re-establish a presence as a bookie after so many bettors had lost their money, which was confiscated.

A homeless veteran lived in the woods near a bicycle trail. Not so unusual, except this homeless veteran was not an

American. He was Russian, and hardly spoke a word of English.

He was a veteran of the Russian War in Afghanistan, where they

fought the Mujahedeen from 1979-1989. We had to address a

citizens complaint made to a City Councilman, so we had the

veteran in his 50's pack up his camp and move, albeit probably

just to a different more remote location in the woods.

How did a Russian veteran end up living in the woods in

Texas? We will never know.

A woman reported that her apartment had been burglarized,

and it was the second time in just four months. It was difficult

for me to look at her. Her face was hideously scarred/disfigured

from what I presumed to have been fire or acid, but she had an

otherwise flawless body. I took her information, and

commented that it was difficult to see what had been disturbed

because there were so many things that had not been put away

(rather than call it a mess). She apologized and commented

that her boyfriend was lazy, didn't do anything around there,

and that she needed to get rid of him. Rightly or wrongly, I
thought to myself that her boyfriend was using her to get an
apartment, and that she was at a tremendous disadvantage at
finding a boyfriend and didn't have the luxury of being choosy.
I sensed that she didn't want me to leave, always coming up
with another question to continue and extend our conversation.
I spoke to her politely and treated her with respect, and I
supposed that she was mostly stared at and shunned by people,
and lonely. I finally left, telling her that we were swamped with
calls (we were) and I needed to get back to work.

   I felt sorry for her, a truly nice person who most people never
gave a chance.

   According to witnesses also waiting for a red light to change,
an older man waiting in another car became impatient. He just
gunned it and rapidly accelerated, attempting to "thread the
needle" between cars passing by in front of him. He didn't
make it, and his car was t-boned. He ended up in the hospital

because he couldn't spare an extra minute of waiting. He was

an attorney running late for an appointment. I had to work the

wreck.

A man was awakened at 2 A.M. by a phone call. The caller

asked him if he was "Scott Smith, the son of Dr. Smith"?

"Yes, I am". "Your father killed my father! I'll hound you to the

grave! Watch your back! I'll see you rot in Hell!", then

slammed down the phone. The man was understandably

shaken by this and wanted a record of it, so I typed up a quick

Incident Report.

I just walked into the station to begin my shift when an

officer asked me if I could take a report from a woman waiting

in the lobby because his shift was over. I obliged him, and

asked her how I could help her. She told me that an older

cousin had raped her repeatedly between the ages of 3 and 10, and then once again when she was 16 years old. I asked if this happened in Dallas, and she replied yes. I gleaned all of the needed information from her, some of which was difficult for her to describe. She was emotionally strong, and her eyes only watered a couple of times. She said the entire family now knew and supported her going to the police. This last rape occurred 6 years before, but the statute of limitations was 10 years from your 18th birthday. Her cousin/suspect had contacted her recently and told her that he had to deal with his demons, and now she had to deal with hers. She was shocked at his indifference and coldness, seeing as how he was the reason why she had a nervous breakdown years ago. She spent some time in a mental hospital to recuperate. I assured her that she was strong and was doing the right thing, and wished her luck in what was to come. I gave her the report number for the Aggravated Sexual Assault report that I was going to do, and told her which of the Child Abuse detectives was going to be handling her case.

Later I tried to type up the report, but I couldn't get past the first page. The computer wouldn't accept the address that she had provided me. A comment appeared at the bottom of the screen that read "DC, not Dallas. After confirming that DC meant Dallas County as in unincorporated, the report needed to be done by a Dallas County Sheriff Deputy. The complainant's new phone number which I had was not to be connected for a few days. However, I had her mother's phone number too. I spoke to the mother and conveyed to her what had happened, and that her daughter needed to unfortunately repeat everything she had told me to a Dallas County Sheriff's Deputy to make the report. The mother said that she had called about loud music a month earlier and Sheriff's Deputies responded. She told her daughter this as well, but she still reported her case to the wrong jurisdiction.

I responded to a bank regarding two male forgery suspects still at the scene. An undercover Deployment officer was nearby and arrived first, but not wanting to reveal his identity watched from outside in his car and didn't enter the bank. As soon as I stepped into the front door I was in a narrow hallway with the two forgery suspects walking toward me. One of them said "Excuse us officer". "You're not leaving" I replied. There was a tense stare down for a long 30 seconds. They both exuded fear. I could hear on my police radio that two Deployment officers were discussing what I was doing. When one replied that I was doing nothing, just standing inside the door with two males, the other officer quickly and correctly surmised that I was blocking the door so the suspects couldn't leave and to get in there and help me. This undercover officer did so shortly followed by the other officer responding to this call.

I'm sure that the two suspects also heard the radio conversation, but given my size and I believe my officer presence, they were reluctant to challenge me. Both suspects surrendered and were arrested.

Officers drove code 3 to a cutting, where a man had been cut up badly when his girlfriend used a broken beer bottle to shred the back of his neck and back. An undercover officer spotted a woman matching the suspect description walking on a major street and saw her board a NB public bus. He followed the bus and noticed her step off a few miles up the road. He continued driving but couldn't discern where she had gone. I was the nearest officer and went to that intersection. In case she was seen by someone going NB, she crossed the street to take a SB bus and sat down on a bus shelter bench. Unknown to her, I observed her do this. She believed she had eluded capture. As I drove toward her, I could see that she was smiling and talking on her phone, no doubt bragging how she really took care of her boyfriend for whatever he did, and how her travel prowess facilitated her escape. Her smug look of confidence changed instantly when she saw me stop my police cruiser. I walked into her midst, had her stand up, and handcuffed her for Aggravated

Assault. Her facial expressions had gone from smiling and laughter, to shock and crying in less than 20 seconds.

Some officers were following a vehicle that had been stolen in a residential burglary from an adjacent suburb. When they were near other officers who were enroute to help with the take down, they turned on their emergency lights for a felony traffic stop. When we arrived, I ran over and handcuffed one suspect who was lying on the road on his stomach. The three face-down suspects were all cuffed, and placed in different police cruisers.

Eventually, the young owner (aged 20) arrived to take custody of his recovered stolen vehicle. By coincidence, the felony stop had happened in front of the house of the best-known Dallas investigative reporter. A crowd of about 15 neighbors had gathered to watch, and she was among them. I saw an opportunity to get a chuckle from a captive audience, so I told the young man reclaiming his vehicle "Now, we did find some marijuana in the car and we're assuming that it belonged to one of the suspects?" His meek reply was "It did", followed by smiles and a few chuckles from the spectators.

I returned from Germany where I had met a friend of a friend named "Gambino" who was in the restaurant business. The very first traffic stop I made upon returning to Dallas was a motorist named "Gambino", also in the restaurant business.

I bring this up to underscore and highlight the prevalence of coincidences. Sometimes innocent people are in the wrong place at the wrong time, and they or their car match the description of a suspect in the same area. Let the police officers do their job and determine that you are not the suspect. A police dragnet sometimes drags in the wrong person. Be conscious of this fact and cooperate, we will sort it out.

A woman from a Drug/Alcohol Rehab center saw a large man enter a backyard from an alley, then break a window of a house and crawl inside. The other officer on the call went to the Rehab Center to get the precise house from the caller, and I went to the street on which the house was located. The other officer broadcasted that it was seven houses down from the corner, and I informed the dispatcher of the correct address. Another officer showed up and went to the rear broken window while I watched the front.

The suspect peered out a front window and saw me. Seconds later, the rear officers pulled the suspect to the ground and cuffed him when he stuck his head out the window. They unknowingly placed him on a fire ant mound, and one of the officers was bit several times on his arm. They called the homeowner from a front yard sign. The home was vacant and the owner was looking for a renter, not a squatter.

The homeowner was grateful and wanted to buy a holiday ham for the Reporting Person. I gave his phone number to the rehab patient who had called and she was going to donate the ham to the Rehab Center. The suspect went to jail for criminal trespassing.

A woman with a crack habit bought $20 of crack—on credit. She didn't pay her dealer so he kicked in her apartment door and announced "I'm coming in here to take something", then stole her PlayStation II along with three video games. As he walked out, he declared "If you don't get my money, I'll come back and shoot everybody!"

The woman told me that he sold her a piece of soap, thinking that she was too high to know the difference. She said she didn't at the time.

While driving, I noticed a tissue blowing on the middle of the road. I knew that it had to have come from an open window, but maybe it was just an accident. I spotted an open car driver window and kept watching it. Seconds later, a crumpled-up

piece of paper flew out of the window, and then another

Kleenex. I stopped the woman and saw that she had a 10-year-

old daughter in the back seat. I lectured the woman that her

actions were teaching her daughter that littering was okay.

Mom wasn't appreciative of being told how to raise her

daughter. The daughter was of course listening, but not having

the use of logic at that age simply said "Leave me alone!" The

mother then tried to lecture me that instructing her about

parenting and psychology was above my pay grade. She was

amusing herself and smugly believed that she got the best of

me, even after she received a "Littering from a vehicle" ticket.

An officer thought that a suspect he was watching might be a

burglary suspect. The suspect turned his head and noticed the

officer following him slowly in his police cruiser, then took off

sprinting. The officer followed him to an apartment, then called

for backup as he stood at a corner to watch the door and the two sides of the apartment that had windows. Cover officers

arrived. After repeated knocks, there was no answer, so we had

a complex manager bring the key. The key only opened one

lock, but the deadbolt was still thrown from the inside. I

stepped up thinking that I was going to be the door kicker, but

another officer took that excitement from me and did the

honors. The door flew open on his second kick, and a middle-

aged man was just inside the front door sitting on a couch and

watching TV. He was quickly put on the carpet while the

original officer and I scurried up a narrow spiral staircase with

weapons drawn and announced "Dallas Police!" We searched

the bedroom, closets, and a bathroom. The suspect had

somehow given us the slip. The other officer started back down

the staircase, but I decided to open one side door of a standard

sized bathroom sink cabinet. The light switch didn't work and I

didn't have a flashlight on me as a day shift officer. I focused

intensely in the dark, and saw a tan toned color object inside. I

thought that I was looking at some towels as my eyes tried to

discern the object by shape. Then I saw a small, round, dime-sized… Hey! That's a nipple! The suspect was scrunched up inside the small cabinet! I yelled "Get out of there! Show me your hands!" The other officer came running back up the staircase and we pulled him out by his hands and cuffed him.

We knew that he was lying about his name, and told him that he would be fingerprinted at the jail. We found his true name and now he had given himself an alias, but he had no warrants. He was charged with Evading Detention and Failure to ID. He had run without a reason, fueling the officer's belief that he was a burglary suspect.

I towed a car that had a broken driver window and a flat tire because I had stickered it for a tow two weeks earlier. The contents of the car for the wrecker sheet inventory: a blanket, two boards, and a very large pink stuffed bunny rabbit.

I was on the way to jail with a prisoner when I happened to pass another Dallas Officer in a police car who also had a prisoner. I moved over into his lane so that he was now behind me as we both got on the entrance ramp to a freeway. As we merged onto the Freeway, another Dallas police car with a prisoner was coming up the right lane and got between us, so that we were now three police cars in a row, all with prisoners heading to jail. The timing was uncanny. To me it underscored how busy Dallas Police could be with fighting crime. We were all involved in unrelated, separate arrests.

We relieved two officers at Parkland Hospital who were watching a 38-year-old prisoner in the ER. He had hit his 80-year-old mother in the head with a pipe and led police in a chase with his kidnapped wife and child in a stolen car. After he slowed down he struck a pole, injuring himself facially with a long laceration on his forehead. It took several police officers to take him into custody because he was hyped up on PCP. In the

ER room he sat up (with wrists and ankles tied down to the bed rails) and said "Wait a minute! I need to see if I'm still here!" (still obviously under the influence of "Angel dust"). He was also very concerned because he thought his penis looked crooked. After the sedative wore off, he arose from his sleep and asked us for one of our guns. If he didn't get one, he'd take us both out. He was an amusing guy that looked like Charles Manson, skinny with bushy, wild uncombed hair, and tattoos on his arms. Since we didn't give him a gun, he thought maybe we could give him a knife so he could cut his gauze restraints on his gurney. Even though he had promised to take care of us if we helped him out, he didn't get a knife.

When he had a room approved, we all settled in and the arrestee pretended to spit at the doctor and a nurse, not winning himself any favors among the medical staff. In fact, they tightened his gauze straps so that he couldn't move his limbs at all while lying on his back.

We were relieved by other officers not long afterwards. As
we were walking away, he told us that he wanted his dick back
(it had a catheter in it), and that we had better not give him the
wrong one.

I did a traffic stop on a vehicle because a license plate check
on my laptop computer showed warrants belonging to a male,
and a male was driving. They were for him. Not many people
can say that they were arrested during a rare Dallas blizzard.

A man and his girlfriend allowed a 20-year-old female friend
to live with them for about six months. She moved out, but
returned to visit and asked to borrow his car just to get some
cigarettes at 10 p.m. on a Thursday Night. Sunday morning, she
still hadn't returned, and he was moving to Florida soon. A few
times, she had teased him by pulling his car up to his apartment
and honked the horn. When he came outside to get his car, she
would let him get close but then laugh and rapidly accelerate.

A 17-year-old girl had just got married and her new husband was shipping out with the U.S. Army the very next day. While they were gone, someone used a key to come inside their apartment and stole their T.V., CD player, social security card, Texas ID card, Visa card, a blue and pink shower curtain, and some of her clothes.

Her brother called her to tell her that he knew who had stolen all of her property because he had found all of it. It was all in his house where their own mother had put it.

I was in a courtroom testifying on an assault case. It was a TBC case (Trial before court- no jury), and only 8 total people were in the courtroom. We had all just returned from lunch. During my testimony, the Defense Attorney's cell phone sounded off in his shirt pocket with a musical chime. Being offended by the negligent interruption, the Judge chimed in and said "That'll cost you 50!"

Paramedics had called the police regarding an attempt suicide victim. I arrived to find the paramedics still standing outside the front door. They said that neighbors had seen the man step outside his apartment and scream with blood on his chest. He was now inside his locked apartment. I told them that I would kick in the door, and then took a step back. A moment before my right leg thrusted forward toward that door, a paramedic said that he thought that he had heard someone on the other side of it. I hesitated, then the door opened and the man was now wearing a dark blue sweatshirt. He removed it when told and several knife tip stab wounds were evident. We found a 7-inch blade knife in the kitchen sink with the front tip having dried blood on it. The complainant confirmed that it was the knife that he had used to hurt himself. As he stood to be handcuffed, he urinated in his sweatpants and a steady flow of it seeped through to trickle and pool on the carpet. The other officer didn't notice this happen, so I waited until the man

was in HIS police cruiser before I told him. We transported the

self-inflicted stab wound victim to Parkland Hospital, where he

would be examined, and given X-rays and other tests in the

Emergency Room area. This took all day, and when I returned

to the station at the end of my shift I had only answered a total

of 1 call.

I started work on one July 3 and was told to relieve some

officers on a beat in my sector. They had not been there long

and it was time for them to go home. I pulled up the comments

on the way there, and saw that the original officers had

responded to a call of a man slumped over the steering wheel.

Paramedics had arrived first and the male driver was

unresponsive with his head down and canted to the right. They

arrived and felt his carotid artery for a pulse, but found none.

They had to put the car in park, as the right front tire had been

stopped by the street curb. When a fireman had gone to the

passenger side of the white van, he saw that the driver had a bullet hole in his right forehead/temple. A neighbor five houses away had been awakened by two gun shots at 1 a.m., 6 hours before this call.

The deceased driver was a man in woman's clothing, wearing makeup, with a makeup case in his van. This led to much speculation as to the events prior to the shooting. I was put on special assignment there the entire day, partly to complete the call and partly to assuage any fears citizens had in this normally quiet peaceful neighborhood.

A 71-year-old woman answered the front door to see a pretty blonde woman in her twenties standing outside. The young woman said hello and said that she was new to the neighborhood and the belt on her vacuum cleaner broke. She tried to borrow a vacuum cleaner from the two guys that lived next door (there really were two guys who lived next door), but they weren't home. When the senior citizen asked the young woman where she lived she said "just two houses down and back a little". The woman brought her the vacuum cleaner, and was told that it won't be needed for long because she's just vacuuming a hardwood floor.

The $200 vacuum cleaner was never seen again.

A woman parked her car in front of the apartment community mailbox, leaving her keys in the ignition; she was only going to be a minute. As she was sorting her mail she glanced at her car and saw a woman trying to get her car in gear. She ran over to her car but the thief backed up and drove away. This is illegal for that reason.

A Texaco employee called police after noticing that a woman had parked in the lot for twenty-five minutes and appeared to be sniffing something. The other officer arrived first and saw her outside her driver door urinating or having just completed. I arrived and watched the woman outside of her truck and told her to just stand there while the officer searched her vehicle. She was catatonic and oblivious. We found an open gallon of Tolulol (Toluene) and a thick stack of paper towels, ideally suited for absorbing sufficient Tolulol before it evaporated. The woman was high from "huffing", or inhaling the paint thinner fumes. She had slurred speech and was mostly incoherent. I had to physically restrain her by holding her arm because she kept wanting to get back into her truck while the other officer was finishing his search.

At first we were going to take her to Detox for Public Intoxication and handcuffed her. She didn't want to willingly enter the backseat to be transported, so we had to shove and push her because she didn't want to sit down. Finally, I was able to close the back door before she could force her leg outside again. We phoned her father because he worked a short distance away, and decided we would release her into his custody if he was willing to take her. Her dad arrived and was obviously disappointed with his daughter; she had a problem with huffing and couldn't quit. She tried once and the best she could do was stay away from it for three months. The fresh air was doing her some good and she was becoming lucid again. She cried with her dad present and said that other addicts had support groups like Al-Anon (AA), but there was nothing for people like her for treatment. I wrote her a ticket for Public Intoxication and released her to her dad. When I handed her the citation to sign, I saw that her finger had just left her nose and she was rolling a big green booger between her thumb and forefinger. I said "That's Gross!" "I know", she replied, and signed the ticket with that same hand after I had her wipe her fingers on her pants.

    She received a free city issued pen along with her ticket copies.

A young mother asked me if when she used the HOV (High-Occupancy Vehicle) lane (encourages car pooling) when there has to be at least two people in the car "Does a baby count?"

I sent out a message on my computer relating to a call that I had just answered, enabling officers in my patrol division to read it and have a chuckle:

"Confucius say woman who go to motel to party & smoke crack with men known only as CC and Coo-Coo and pass out, will wake up to find that her purse and car gone."

Her stolen car was worth $15,000.00.

Driving down a street adjacent to White Rock Lake, I spied what appeared to be a dead owl or a dead hawk on the right side of a traffic lane, and motorists were steering around it so as to not hit it. I U-turned at the next small intersection and returned curious to inspect this unknown bird of prey. I stopped my police cruiser behind the bird on the quiet road and turned on my emergency lights, then walked over to the carcass. The wings were spread, and the bird's head was obscured as it laid face down. To get a better look at it, I nudged it with my right foot and was surprised that it actually moved on its own. As I tried to make a phone contact with a rescue organization or a Game Warden, the Red-Tailed Hawk stood up wobbly, still looking stunned. It apparently had been hit by a passing car as it swooped to land at a nearby squirrel road kill. After about 10 minutes, the hawk started to react to passing cars by turning its head. Within 5 more minutes, it launched itself and flew off into the woods just 10 yards away.

When I finally contacted my Game Warden friend, I learned that hawks and owls are commonly only stunned when struck by a moving car while in flight, and often only appear to be dead.

Some Officers are timid and unaggressive when they need to be otherwise. If you allow a suspect to disrespect you without putting him in his place, he could easily construe that as a sign to verbally abuse or disrespect the next officer.

A co-worker was riding her bike talking to another cyclist alongside her on the bike trail. A bicyclist on a racing bicycle approached them from behind. Rather than simply go onto the grass briefly to go around them, or use the roadway, or simply say "on your left" to have them move over for him so that he could pass by, he rudely said "Get out of the way you fucking idiots!" This cyclist knew that she was a police officer because her back had a wide white horizontal strip in it with the word "POLICE" in bold black letters. She called me after she stopped him to ask what she could do about it. I told her to write him a citation for "Profanity in the park", a city ordinance violation.

I was confounded and disappointed when she told me later that she just gave him a warning. In effect, insinuating "I'll let you call me a fucking idiot this time, but the next time I'm going to write you a ticket."

I rode my police bicycle up to some bleachers at a baseball field in the park. The game was over, but a number of people lingered. There was an open cooler filled with beer, but of course no one claimed it; alcohol in a Dallas Park is illegal, and they all knew it. The only person near it was a 12-year-old girl, and it certainly wasn't hers. I personally opened and dumped about 35 cans of beer. I'm sure some of them weren't very happy about that, but no one had said a word. It still cost less than a $150 ticket.

I drove past a girl at a bus stop on a school day and believed her to be a truant. I made a U-turn and asked her age. "Fourteen." Why aren't you in school?" "I'm on my way now. I slept late." She had a book bag on her back, but I didn't believe her. "Get in the back, I'll take you to school." "But I already bought a bus pass." "Get in" I reiterated.

There was no way any student would miss the first several hours of school and then at 1:45 p.m. take a bus to get there.

In June of 2015, a heavily armed and body armored man shot up Dallas Police HQ with high powered rifles and even exploded some pipe bombs outside the building. Despite hundreds of rounds being expended, no civilians or police officers were injured or killed in the late evening rampage that ended hours later when a SWAT sniper took him out while he was still inside his van.

I worked behind the desk for a couple of hours the next day at my Patrol Division and fielded an incoming civilian call. The older woman said "Officer, I don't want to take up much of your time. I just wanted to say thank you and good job for taking care of that fool!" I knew exactly who she was referring to, and replied "Thank You Ma'am. He is where he needs to be" (dead).

I stopped a woman one night for running a red light and wrote her a ticket. I informed her that she had traffic ticket warrants out of another city. She was surprised and asked me if they could possibly belong to her twin. It was hard to believe that there was a sister who was also 5'5 and 300 lbs. Sure enough, I had erred. No doubt thinking it to be cute, their mother had foolishly given them not only first and middle names that started with the same letter, but first and middle names that were alike phonetically and sounded the same, but were spelled differently.

We were returning from jail when we heard two officers given a call regarding a homicide suspect at a train station wearing a red shirt and green shorts. We added ourselves to the call as we were close and didn't want the homicide suspect to elude capture just because he stepped onto a train. We were the first Dallas Officers there, but we saw that DART

(Transportation) Officers had just taken him into custody. We swapped out handcuffs and took the arrestee to HQ to be fingerprinted.

Apparently on his first arrest, he had no ID and no previous record of arrests. The false name that he had provided to his arresting officers then became his true name from taking his fingerprints, and the true name that he had provided us became an AKA, or an alias. The original fake name that he had given from his earlier arrest was also as a homicide suspect. At first, a Homicide detective thought that he might extract a confession from some hoped-for cooperation from the arrestee, but that didn't happen. It didn't matter. He was still wanted for a fresh Aggravated Robbery warrant with a $100,000.00 bond. He had plenty of time to ponder a long jail term that zero cooperation would bring him. In the meantime, the Homicide detectives just needed more time to build their case. He wasn't going anywhere.

Having driven to a spot where an accident had happened, there were no cars present, only glass residue. I went to my next call involving an alarm, and it was false when a kid met me outside and informed me that he had hit the wrong button. Then he asked me if he needed to call the police because he just had his first accident and just exchanged information with the other driver. Millions of people living in the DFW area, and several dozen Dallas Police officers in the area and I somehow took two related consecutive calls. He had just been involved in that accident.

I arrived at a domestic disturbance and found the woman waiting outside with her two young children. Her husband had shoved her on the couch, choked her, then told her "I ought to kill you bitch!" He chucked a set of keys at her cheek causing it to bleed. The suspect was still inside the apartment. I had the woman and children remain outside. My cover officer hadn't arrived yet, but I decided to enter the apartment anyway knowing that he couldn't be too far away (we impatiently did that a lot years ago). I unholstered my weapon and searched the apartment, announcing my presence. It appeared deserted, and all was quiet. I routinely opened a closet door and had a fright. There sitting atop a dryer was my suspect. He had no weapon and exited the closet as instructed and I handcuffed him.

Just a week earlier, there was a Dallas Police Officer who was killed when he and others entered an apartment to run a warrant. The officer had merely opened a closet door. When he did, the suspect who had been inside hiding killed him instantly with a shotgun blast to the face.

I arrested a DWI and after he chose a blood draw over a breathalyzer test sample, I dropped his blood test tubes into the drop box, and wrote down the arrestee's name of "Flores" in the logbook. The name immediately preceding having been arrested for DWI the same night was also "Flores."

One overnight shift or "1st watch" as it is called in Dallas, NE patrol where I worked had 3 unrelated homicides. Somehow that information and any suspect information was not passed along to the day shift officers who were starting their shift and just had their detail (briefing). I happened to have heard it from an academy classmate who had just ended his 1st watch shift. That was an egregious example of an officer safety discrepancy and poor communications; we hadn't heard anything about the 3 murders or murderers from the previous shift in our morning detail (roll call).

I responded to a burglary of an aquarium store. We found the front door glass broken and the alarm sounding. We searched the store but found no one. As we were about to walk back out the front, I rushed to the back room because it sounded like someone was walking thru water making plopping sounds with his feet as he walked. It turned out to be a dozen fish that had flipped out of their aquariums and were flopping

on the puddles of a wet floor.

A man was trying hard to flirt with a woman in a convenience

store. She was polite but tried not to seem interested, and

ignored him the best she could. He left before her and she

didn't notice his vehicle. When she returned to her vehicle, she

saw that he had left her a parting souvenir-- a Polaroid picture

of his penis on her front seat.

A woman in a bikini was drinking beer while she was driving,

weaving recklessly and believed to have been drunk. A man

was following and reported her to 911. She had already

sideswiped a parked car on the shoulder of the freeway. We

took the call and actually found the woman and arrested her for

DWI.

The "woman wearing a bikini" comment that was reported was far from what I had envisioned in my imagination.

A teenaged girl worked at a cigarette store and just before 9 a.m., she walked out to her car with a bank bag, about to make a deposit of about $2500 cash and many personal checks. When she was at her car door, she sensed a shadow come over her and suddenly the bank bag was ripped from her hand and she was shoved up against her car. The robbery suspect ran off, leaving the girl behind with a bruise on her arm.

Unbeknown to the robber, an undercover officer had just witnessed the entire crime. The officer happened to be in the same mini-mall parking lot to drop off some vacation film for processing at a drug store. The officer broadcasted his observations as he followed the running suspect and watched him climb into a nearby pickup truck. Within blocks, patrol officers had the car stopped. The robber bailed on foot but was soon captured. The money was returned to the business even before the punk knew how much he had; the cash and checks were still rubber-banded. The girl was expectedly shaken, and told us that she had only worked for the business one week and that they already had two shoplifters and now this robbery (it WAS a bad neighborhood). While we were still in the store, she contacted the home office. They suggested to her that maybe all of these events in just one week were more than a coincidence, insinuating that she must be involved. Riled by the remark and insult, she quit on the spot. Personally, I didn't think that she was an accomplice.

A veteran police officer had parked his car in a parking garage and used the vertical valet service belt to go down through the garage levels. As he was descending, the step he was standing on was believed to have broken, causing him to fall and dangle upside down with his foot caught in the chain. A nearby officer rushed to assist him after he screamed for help, as did a parking lot attendant, but they could not hold his weight to pull him out of his predicament. When somebody else who was unaware of the accident pulled on the chain from a different level to try and get it to move again, the officer's foot came loose and he plunged to his death three stories below. Upside down, his death was immediate.   A freakish accident.

Another officer and I worked in the patrol division that was closest to his suburban home. We were assigned to go there and pick up his 12-year-old daughter who was at the house alone and deliver her to grandma's house in Dallas. When we arrived, I introduced ourselves to the daughter and told her that her dad had been in a serious accident and that we needed to bring her to her grandma's. The responsible, stoic girl quickly let the dog out, set the house alarm, and climbed into the back seat. It was evident that she was very worried about her dad and this had to be the toughest, most stressful time in her young life. She sat quietly in her own thoughts the entire ride. We felt compassion and pitied her for the devastating news that she was about to receive upon her arrival.

I finished taking a BMV (Burglary of a Motor Vehicle) report from a grandmother, and I saw that her 4-year-old grandson had a large smile on his face. He had started using his many crayons at the kitchen table as soon as I walked inside, and now his picture was complete. He got excited and said "It's Ginormous!", and proudly handed me his drawing as I stepped outside the front door. It portrayed me holding a giant multicolored pistol as big as me in the picture with a bullet (more like an artillery shell) coming out of the barrel.

I still have that picture.

Some homeowners were going through things in their attic to throw away and came across some U.S. savings bonds that belonged to the previous owners. At first, they thought that there was no way that the owners could've forgotten about them and they just must not have been redeemable and threw them in the trash. They had second thoughts and called the

police.

I'd never owned a U.S. savings bond, but there were no

signatures and they also appeared to me to be unredeemed. I

put them into the police property room as found property.

There were 50 series EE $1000 U.S. savings bonds, and 28 series

E $50 savings bonds.

I made a U-turn on a car that I thought had a 3-year expired

inspection sticker. Sure enough it was expired, and I wrote him

a ticket. As I started to walk back to my cruiser, he said "Officer,

I just have one thing to say" and I expected to hear something

derogatory when I returned. Instead, he added "I just wanted

to thank you for being the only one out here doing your job",

obviously an overstatement. He said 3 years prior he had

ventured into a suburb to get his inspection sticker, but his car

had failed. He hadn't even driven a mile when an officer from

that city pulled him over and wrote him a ticket. He had been in

Dallas ever since driving with that expired inspection sticker,

and I was the only officer to ever stop him for it. I told him

officers in Dallas had more to do and didn't always have time

for citations. He told me he thought that a lot of officers just

didn't want to enforce traffic laws. I had to smile because I

agreed.

Seldom does a motorist praise an officer for writing him a

ticket.

A downstairs neighbor heard running water from the

bathroom above her bathroom for many hours and called the

police. We arrived and had someone from the office let us into

the apartment to do a welfare check, as the male tenant was

elderly. We found the man naked, his legs out of the bathtub,

but lying on his back in the bathtub. He was deceased and

either had a heart attack and fell, or slipped and fell, grabbing

and tearing the shower curtain off some of its O-rings as he

went down. Strangely, he had fallen and came to rest with his face a foot under the water spigot, and the bath water poured directly into his open mouth with his eyes still open. Was he dead before he landed in the bathtub or did he drown? The Medical Examiner had him transported to the M.E. office to find out.

A mother had called the police about her large unruly 20-year-old son who was angry and threatening her. Another officer who was also 6'3" and 220 pounds arrived and we went to the back bedroom where the totally deaf son was sitting on his bed. He stared and sneered intensely at his mother when she explained to us what had happened. He was mumbling incoherently and using sign language that was directed at his mother. I asked her what he was signing, and she replied "He's telling me that he's going to kick my ass". He continued signing the same gestures. When his sister stepped into the doorway, I asked her what her brother was saying. "He's telling my mom that he's going to fuck her up". I told him to stand up and put his hands behind his back, and mom warned "He'll probably fight you!' Luckily for him, he cooperated though still exhibited his attitude problem.

At the jail, I had the judge sign an extra 24 hour hold and an Emergency Protective Order. The mother had told us that the family had just moved to Dallas from Oklahoma, and lately she had been calling the police a couple times each week about her son's anger management issues.

I have met some intelligent people who are somehow not good at spelling. Many years ago, I saw a BOLO (Be On the Lookout) vehicle message come across the laptop computer screen that began with "Just stolin". Of all the words for a police officer to misspell. Embarrassed for him, after seeing it misspelled on three separate occasions, I sent him a correction message.

We had orange 24 hr. stickers that we used to put on vehicles to compel the owners to move them from the public street when they had obviously been motionless for a long time (flat tire, etc.) I noticed once that the orange warning sticker that I had used said "WARNING! This vechicle may be impounded if it is not removed within 24 hours". Later that day at the station I checked the stack of 24-hour notices, and they all had that same typo. This obviously reflected poorly on the police department, so after a few phone calls I was speaking to the Dallas Printing Room supervisor. He sought out his supply of orange 24-hour notices and laughed, saying that he never noticed. I assumed that in short order we would receive a fresh supply of corrected stickers to spare us any further humiliation or ridicule from any observant citizens. It didn't happen; we didn't get a fresh batch until the misspelled supply was exhausted.

New Police Chiefs always implement some changes that they think will benefit the police department. Most people want their police officers to take illegal guns and drugs off the street. Indeed, police officers have their monthly police work tabulated as a way to measure up their work ethic to compare them to other officers for calls, arrests, tickets, guns, drugs. One of our new Chiefs decided during his short tenure that police officers would no longer get "activity" credit for seizing guns and drugs from criminals, which logically didn't go over very well with the rank and file street cops fighting crime every day.

A woman parked her pickup truck in the middle of the drive of a park parking lot, blocking access to a boat ramp. Just as I wondered what kind of dimwit would park there, a boater tried to back and maneuver his boat trailer around the truck, but he just gave up and drove away to find another boat ramp somewhere. I drove over and stepped out of my squad car to peer inside. There was one occupant, a 1 ½ year old baby sleeping in a child safety seat on the back seat of the vehicle. I looked around, but saw no one. Finally, after a long 10 seconds, a woman scurried over from about 40 yards away. She said she had only left the baby alone for several minutes, but she only needed to leave the baby unattended for at least five minutes to be in violation, and received a citation. She admitted that she had "made a poor decision".

I pulled alongside a 7th grader at 9:30 a.m. on a school day. I asked "Why are you not in school today?" "I'm absent", came his reply. No fooling. I took the genius back to school.

I was getting into position near a home that was targeted for a narcotics raid. I had to cover the rear from the alley, and thought I would be in a better position if I went over a waist high chain-link fence with dense horizontal vines growing all across the top. I placed my left hand on top of the fence to hoist myself over by swinging to the right, but stopped moving when my left hand was stuck. Hidden under the foliage, the

metal barbs at the top of the chain link were not turned over

like most, and were just sticking up like a big X. I punctured my

hand on the metal barbs. Here the raid hadn't even begun and I

already needed to go to the hospital for treatment and a

tetanus shot, which I did afterwards.

On a 90-degree day in July, I drove into a park where men

were playing baseball. I spied three men holding large7-11

coffee cups near the bleachers. Drinking hot coffee on a 90

degree day in July at 3 p.m.? I walked over to look into one

man's cup and he pulled it towards his chest confirming my

suspicions. They were drinking beer from those coffee cups,

knowingly violating the park prohibition on alcohol, believing

their ploy would fool police. Maybe it did for a while, but that

day they received Alcohol in the Park tickets, and poured the

beer from their coffee cup.

Texas experiences a drought periodically. During one, the water level at Lake Ray Hubbard (owned by Dallas) was down several feet. Some kids were wading in shallow water that would've normally been over their heads. They stepped on and found 6 pistols on the lakebed. They were there for who knows how many years, and were apparently thrown from shore by someone for an unknown reason. All were very rusted except the chrome one, which still had a near legible serial number. They all went to the police property room.

Though there are many gay bars, some men are bisexual and married, and haven't come "out-of-the-closet" for that reason. They prefer to keep their sexuality private and a secret from their wives, and so some will seek out anonymous male sex partners in public parks. Well aware of this, I noticed just two cars in a park parking lot and both were unoccupied. I decided to investigate and get out of my car to locate the owners. On the partly wooded Flagpole Hill, I walked to the rear and saw two males. They hadn't yet seen me, so I crouched down behind some bushes to observe their actions. They both looked around, then unzipped their pants to expose their penises and began to masturbate each other. I emerged from my hiding spot and announced "I need to see your ID!" They were visibly shocked as you can imagine, and both twisted and turned a few moments to gather their senses. Both decided to run, albeit in opposite directions. I started to run after the male that subsequently ran down the hill, across six lanes of Northwest Highway traffic and into the woods, but decided to go back and instead pursue the male who had fled back to the parking lot. I arrived there just as he was driving away, and radioed his vehicle description and travel direction. Fortunately, an undercover officer was just down that same road and waited for the suspect to pass him so that he could follow. Other officers made the traffic stop, and I came to identify and arrest him for Public Lewdness.

The other male hid in the woods for hours. A canine officer brought his German Shepherd to the forest but decided that there were too many mosquitoes for his dog (translation: too many mosquitoes for him). The escaped male had a rental car in the parking lot. Days later I phoned the rental car company to get information on the driver, but was disappointed to discover that the vehicle had been returned from that time period by a driver of a different race.

A woman used an ATM, then went to a Walmart Store where she pushed around her shopping cart with an expensive designer purse in the child seat. She had noticed a teenager loitering nearby. He saw his opportunity and ran over and swiped the purse, though it must have been heavier than he thought because he dropped it. The purse owner caught up to him and grabbed the back of his shirt, but he picked up the purse and continued his escape. He ran into the parking lot and jumped into a waiting Ford Tempo. Another accomplice also entered the vehicle, and they fled.

The complainant's shopping spree never began. She had just withdrawn $5000.00 from the ATM, far more than the suspects expected, unless they saw her use the ATM and followed her from the bank.

A woman allowed a man to come into her apartment so that she could trim his facial hair. The man insulted her for no reason and she queried him about his persistent need to always hurl insults at her and told him to leave. The man continued using epithets and used his big belly to shove her. The woman tried to call 911, but he slapped the phone from her hands and again he used his belly to push and jostle her. He used his belly weight to hold her down on a bench trying to prevent her escape. She squeezed past him and slipped out of his belly hold and went outside to shout for help. The man used his protruding belly one more time, and thrust his stomach to bounce her against a railing outside her door, then departed.

The woman had known the suspect for decades and he had a history of verbal and physical abuse. He recently told her that he had heard about someone that tried to hire a hit man to kill a spouse and if he had the money he would hire one to take care of her mother.

Oddly, the male suspect had recently had a mastectomy for breast cancer.

An aggravated robbery victim came by the police station to tell police that he had seen the suspect in a vacant apartment a few miles away. I informed the dispatcher of my destination and had another officer go there to meet me. I went to the complex office to verify that the apartment was vacant and to retrieve the key. We unlocked one door to the apartment but found it to barricaded by a refrigerator on the inside. I pushed hard on the door and the refrigerator toppled over onto the floor making a loud slamming noise. We rushed in with weapons drawn yelling "Police!" We found no males in the apartment, just two stark naked females who were trying to keep cool with a ceiling fan from the muggy 90 degree outside temperature. One female had just flushed the toilet, probably to flush drugs. We had the women put their clothes on and the manager gave them a criminal trespass warning. They had no warrants.

The property owner was hoping to sell this dilapidated complex, but it was in a bad neighborhood and he was having trouble finding a buyer. He had been too strict with prospective tenants given the bad area and the apartments were only 30% occupied. This left many vacant apartments for unpaid lodging when a trespasser forced open a door or window.

I stopped a woman for speeding, and as I approached her driver door she held out her New York DL with a Dallas address (she must've worked/lived in two states). Even before I had said a word, she told me "I just want to tell you right now that there's a typo on my address and it's incorrect." I saw it immediately. Instead of reading "Poppy" drive, it read "Poopy" drive.

I arrived for my Sam's Club job and an employee quickly told me that there was a ½ naked woman far out in the parking garage lot. The employee lead the way and I found the drunk woman. She was not bruised or injured, but was crying and said "They tried to kill me! Kill me! Shoot Me!" She was only wearing a bra and an open blouse. Her panties, one shoe, her purse, and a car mat were lying next to her. She said they had dumped her out of their car onto the parking lot. Paramedics arrived and put a sheet over her to modestly cover her, then placed her in their ambulance where she passed out. She was so intoxicated that they could not even revive her with smelling salts. They transported her to a hospital for observation.

I believed her to be a drug addicted prostitute. She had two seven-year-old checkbooks in her cluttered purse and no longer lived at her DL address which was in a better part of town.

Working a side security job at a Sam's store, I noticed a man and his two teen-aged sons looking toward the ceiling while they were in a check-out line. There were about 30 people checking out at the registers. I read the lips of one who mouthed the words "Where are the cameras?" After they finished buying their merchandise, they walked the thirty yards or so to the exit door where I was standing in uniform. I commented to them "They're here. We have them." They looked at each other quizzically. I repeated "We have them. The cameras." They were all dumbfounded and embarrassed that I knew what they had been talking about and left the store without saying a word.

I covered another officer on a traffic stop. A traffic violation led to a routine check of the driver DL and he had warrants, so he was going to jail. The woman in the car volunteered that she also had unpaid ticket warrants. She was his wife and wanted to be with him at the jail. After all, they had just been married earlier that same day by a Justice of the Peace. We took them both to jail. For better or for worse.

Two days before Christmas, I got a call about a man who was crying outside in an apartment breezeway in a light rain. He was supposedly crying as he went back and forth from his apartment. Had tragedy struck? Had someone died in his apartment? Did he just receive bad news? Nope. When I arrived, I spotted him and walked toward him and his presumed girlfriend. They were standing on a complex sidewalk together. Crying , he was wearing shorts, one black slipper, and one black dress shoe. I heard him say that he loved the world. He saw me and started walking toward me with open arms and said

"Officer! I love you!" I did what any compassionate,

sympathetic officer would have done in the same situation; I

backed up and said "Don't touch me!" The man replied "Okay."

I asked the woman (his wife) if she knew what was happening.

She replied that he was fine, that he just had something positive

happen in his life. I assumed that he had become pious and

accepted Jesus Christ into his heart. I addressed him and told

him that it was cold and rainy and he was underdressed, and

people were worried about him. I suggested that he go inside

his apartment to call his friends to share with them the joy of

Christmas. He thought that was a good idea and stepped into

his apartment with his wife. I saw their son inside about aged 4

and I said "Look! There's your son! There's someone you can

hug!" The man said "Oh yes! I love you!" and gave his son a

hug. I added "And your wife! Don't forget to hug her too!" He

replied "Oh yes! I love my wife!" and also gave her a hug.

Having felt like I helped to spread the joy of Christmas, my

work was done, and I moved on.

A vehicle on LBJ Freeway braked and swerved suddenly resulting in a 5-car accident. I arrived and a fire engine, ambulance, and a county employee were already there, the latter having put down the many orange cones. No one was hurt, and the vehicles all had minor damage. I quickly saw what had caused the accident; there was a dead German Shepherd lying on the left lane. There was quite a bit of his blood trailed on the pavement, and a sprayed blood pattern on the pavement from a second impact. The scene was calm, so I walked directly to the dead dog to look for a collared I.D. tag, putting on a pair of rubber gloves that I kept in my ballistic vest pocket as I walked. They had dried and ripped from age, and a fore finger and thumb became wet with dog blood. I radioed for a streets and sanitation truck to remove the carcass off the Freeway. I had heard that the poor dog had briefly been alive after it was mortally wounded. I could see nearby that a 6-year-old girl in a soccer uniform was being comforted by her mother. I made a few phone calls from the info on the dog tag and saw that the dog's name was "Turk". I could only leave a message for the owner because the line was busy on several tries. The city

sanitation worker arrived in a pick-up truck that was towing a white trailer with a large triangular door on each side. The worker opened one of these doors which revealed a pile of dead animals, including a clearly visible larger German Shepherd. A smart dog breed, but how many dogs know the danger of traffic? The little girl's mother had anticipated the opening door and she had turned her daughter away from the sight which could easily have given her nightmares. The roadkill remover grasped one front and one rear paw of the dog with his gloved hands, then like an Olympic ball and hammer thrower, did a couple of spins and with his centrifugal force, hoisted the dog atop the dead animal carcass pile. Away he drove with the dog collar and tag, bound for the next dead critter.

____

As a bicycle officer, I often stopped at a liquor store on the north end of White Rock Lake to slake my thirst with a cold one—as in a Gatorade or energy drink. While I was there once a man walked in with a boy who was about 13-years-old. The boy didn't remove his dark, wraparound sunglasses and kept

them on as he walked around with his dad inside the store. As the boy walked past me, I said "Hello. Let me ask you something. Have you been here before?" "I have a few times." "Okay. I was wondering. You know your way around pretty good for a blind guy."

The father was following behind him, and as he passed me, he commented for his son "Actually, he is legally blind." Having put my foot in my mouth trying to make a funny wisecrack, I said that I was sorry and didn't say another word.

I was dispatched on a bank robbery. As I was en-route, two other officers informed the dispatcher that they had arrived at the bank. Unluckily for the bank robber, these officers had been eating lunch one building away behind the bank. I arrived and put out a radio description of the suspect, and got witness information. A short time later, an officer had who he believed to be the bank robbery suspect in custody and handcuffed. I brought my four witnesses to his location, and separately, they identified him as being the robber.

The suspect had waited his turn in the bank teller line. When he advanced to the teller window he slid a paper note to the teller that read "This is a robbery. I am armed and have nothing to lose. Please put the money in large bills on the counter. Thank You and God Bless." He never presented a weapon. If he had robbed other banks, he would have been given an FBI moniker like "Gentleman bandit." The teller had read the note and correctly postulated that he was too nice to be a threat; she bravely didn't give him any money. He received nothing at all except an inevitable trip to Federal Prison.

An officer that reviewed and approved accident reports done on "Polaris" software sent out a City wide message to hundreds of Dallas Patrol Officers one evening to be mindful of OUR errors, with a couple of hints to avoid the most common mistakes. I had to chuckle because—ironically-- he wasn't too concerned about his own errors when he reminded us how to avoid making our errors. He typed "another words" instead of "in other words, "and "ledgeable" instead of "legible."

A young male driver was speeding and lost control, spinning off the road and through some grass, and wedged his car between two trees front end forward. Amazingly he was unhurt, and was fortunate to have been stopped just a few yards from a lake, the depth of which would have submerged his vehicle and likely caused him to drown.

I had waited for a red light to change, and when it did, I noticed a car zip past on my left side looking like he was speeding. I caught up to him and paced him at about 15 mph over the speed limit. He didn't slow despite my being in his rear-view mirror, so I did a traffic stop. I approached and commented that he was driving a little too fast for someone who had a police officer behind them. With a strained look on his face, he replied "Yes sir. I have a problem," and showed me a box of Imodium anti-diarrhea tablets. He very quickly showed me his insurance card. My nose sensed that he was telling me the truth. I told him that if it wasn't too late there was a gas station just up the road, and cut him loose.

I stopped a man on a traffic stop who spoke little English. I didn't believe him when he said he had no I.D. on him, so I had him step out of the car and patted his back pants pocket, the bulge being an obvious wallet. I asked him again to give me his ID, and he took his wallet from his pocket and opened it, showing me several empty wallet card holders. I didn't see any ID card for him, but I did see a young blond girl's ID card in his wallet. I asked to see that ID and asked him why someone else's ID was in his wallet. He responded that it was his girlfriend as he handed me her ID. I didn't believe him; she was about 20 years old (much younger than him) and lived in a much different part of town. I took her ID back to my police cruiser to do a "crisscross" on the name and address to obtain her phone number. In short order, I had that phone number sent to me on my screen. I called and one of her parents answered. I introduced myself, and asked if I could speak to her. She was still sleeping but they awakened her and she came to the phone. After framing the situation for her, she was shocked and said that she did not know the driver. She reasoned that the only way that he could have her ID card was that he must have found the ID card that she lost in the Deep Ellum part of Dallas a couple of years back. I commented that he probably had been carrying her ID for that long in his wallet and that he had been telling everyone that she was his girlfriend. It freaked her out a bit. I told her that with her permission I would confiscate it and destroy it, since it had expired and she already had a replacement. She readily agreed

and thanked me.

I was in uniform working a side job. A woman walked to me

carrying a female Chihuahua with obvious milk-swollen teats.

She asked if I could call someone to help the dog. I surmised

that the unknown owner had kept the puppies until they no

long needed to be weaned, then had disposed of the mother

dog by dropping her into a Walmart parking lot trash can. She

heard the dog crying and rescued it. This undisputed friendly

rescue dog was placed in my hands.

Mere minutes later, this high pedestrian traffic area of the

parking garage presented me with a good Samaritan who

happened to be with a Chihuahua Rescue Organization. She

liberated the dog from me to take it to a veterinarian for a

health screening and flea treatment.

A man was seen waving a gun at the rear of an adjacent apartment complex. The other officer and I arrived at the same time. He had called the Reporting Person and the suspect was still on the tennis court wearing a blue jersey with a gold "25" on it. We couldn't miss him with this description.

We walked the apartment complex and found the suspect with his back to us. There were several children playing in our vicinity. We decided to pounce on the suspect from behind and take him by surprise rather than risk a shootout that could harm innocent bystanders, though we saw no weapon at the time. We crept up to the corner of a building and were only ten yards away from him. He was still unaware of our presence. Together, we rushed him with pistols drawn and pounced on him, simultaneously shouting "Police! Get on the ground." He buckled to the ground under our weight and offered no resistance, being taken completely by surprise. He was a big guy who turned out to be just 16 years old and not very bright. I searched his pockets and found the black pistol he had been waving, as well as a silver and black pistol that he had tucked into one of his long socks. They were both realistic-looking BB guns. The kid explained that he was just firing at birds. We revealed to him how his BB guns looked real to other people not just from a distance but also from up close. We divulged to him that he could have been shot by one of us and we would have been justified if he had turned to face us while pointing a BB gun at us. He understood. We went to his Aunt's apartment where he was staying but she was absent. A neighbor knew the boy and his aunt and agreed to hold the two BB pistols until she returned and provide her with an explanation.

The boy was released, having learned a valuable and perhaps a life saving lesson.

Driving through a public parking lot with several other people present, I noticed a dog running around but didn't see an owner. I got out and checked the dog by looking at his collar tag when I heard a voice from a distance say "He's with me." I saw an older man sitting on the open tailgate of his pickup truck and asked him how the dog was with him if he was fifty yards away, and where was his leash? The man held up the leash, but otherwise didn't move. I told him that for public safety we have a leash law and his dog needed to be on a leash. He said "Okay", and I went back to my vehicle and started to drive away. In my rear-view mirror, I saw that the man had put his leash down and was still sitting on his tailgate, still motionless. I circled back and asked for his ID, explaining that he had his warning, failed to heed it, and now he was getting a ticket. Only now he dismounted and called his dog over to him to be leashed, but it was too late for him. After he reluctantly signed his ticket, he commented to me that "We know what this is really about. "What do you mean?""We know what this is really about", he repeated.

Yeah, we do, it's about you being defiant and not listening to a warning. You deserve that ticket. Be sure and take care of it within 21 days."

He was a different race than me and intimated that was why he

had received the ticket.

A woman and a female friend got a ride to their destination

by a cab driver. Instead of paying the cab fare, they decided to

carjack the cab driver of his Yellow Cab. Several miles away, still

speeding away from their crime scene, the suspect/driver lost

control on black ice. The cab spun and slammed into a concrete

pillar below an overpass, killing the passenger. The injured

incapacitated driver went to the hospital until she was

discharged and was then taken to the county jail.

There is now a "Watch for Ice" sign at that accident location

hinged in the middle than can be unfolded/opened during the

winter.

On the 4th of July 1994, I spent the day working at a Lake Ray

Hubbard Road block at the entrance of a park. There were two

large white signs with red letters informing motorists that there was a road block checkpoint for fireworks just ahead. Some vehicles made a U-turn before they drove that far, but most did not. We confiscated three large garbage bags of fireworks during our eight-hour shift working with the Fire Department.

In many cases, if I suspected people of having fireworks in their vehicle, I would tell them that if I had to search their vehicle and then found fireworks, I would confiscate the illegal fireworks and write them a possession of fireworks tickets that could cost up to $2000.00. This was quite effective at getting them to tell the truth. They didn't have to know that I really didn't have probable cause to search their vehicle. Their perceived assumption that I would was enough to coerce honesty from them and prompt them to turn over all or some of their fireworks. A few were very upset with relinquishing a large, or a costly number of fireworks, but no one received a citation that day.

A man called police because his wife was causing a verbal disturbance and wouldn't let him have access to their apartment by locking him out. I arrived and determined that no crime had occurred, and tried to convince his wife to let him inside because he had just as much right to the apartment as she did. She replied that she wasn't going to unlock the door. I checked both of them for warrants, and she was the only one who had outstanding ticket warrants. I inquired about firearms, and the husband assured me that there were none in their apartment. I informed the husband that if he was willing to accept responsibility for the damage, and if he gave me permission, then I would kick in the door and place her under arrest for her warrants. He said yes, so I kicked in the door and arrested his wife. She went to jail, surprised that her husband would allow an officer to force his way in to arrest her. He was happy, and told her that all she had to do was not be so stubborn and just let him inside.

A woman and her boyfriend had some drinks at a bar, then went home and had some more drinks. They ended up in bed watching TV, and she drifted off to sleep. When she awoke at 8 A. M., she tried to rouse him, but she couldn't revive him. He was a recovering heroin addict, though still had a couple of needle marks on an arm. He had also been taking several different medications, including one that had just been filled yesterday but could not be found.

Paramedics took him to a hospital but he died. When I arrived he was already under a white sheet. Given the circumstances coupled with his age, he was transported to the Medical Examiner's office for an autopsy. He was only 21.

Just as our shift started, my rookie and I were given a call regarding a check forgery one block away at a bank. Two forged checks presented earlier in the day had alerted the tellers to be wary of anyone cashing a particular health care company's check. We arrived and upon learning the details, took the waiting 17-year-old girl into custody for having forged her name

to a $1497.00 check and attempting to cash it.

We also arrested a 20-year-old male who had forged a

$1767.00 check and tried to cash it AFTER the bank had already

called police about the forger #1. He had greedily and foolishly

waited when they had asked him to be patient. Both of them

had probably been told some fictitious story by an older adult as

a ruse that they could earn an easy and large fee for signing and

cashing a check, though I doubt they were told the checks had

been stolen. Carelessly naive, they unknowingly committed a

felony. The 20-year- old also had marijuana in his possession

when searched.

Neither had ever been arrested before and became instant

felons.

On another check forgery call, I arrested a 28-year-old man

for trying to cash a forged, stolen $885.00 check at a bank. The

tellers said that he had been nervous when he presented the

forged check, and he should've been; he was actually denied

being allowed to cash a check just one day before and here he

was trying to cash another one AT THE SAME BANK.

At a large electronics store, a man was surveilled on remote

video and was seen removing a $200 phone from its box and

placed it in the box of a $40 phone. He was brought to the loss

prevention office. We arrived, and upon learning that he was

going to jail for Fraudulent Removal, the suspect offered double

whatever the phone cost, or "whatever it takes". He had

enough cash in his wallet to pay for the more expensive phone

but admitted that he was cheap.

A man went to visit the home of a female friend. He spoke to

her through the door for an hour wanting her to open it, or to

step outside so that he could be certain that she was fine. She

told him that she was, but he was suspicious of that assertion

and phoned police. He never saw her and was concerned that

she perhaps was being held against her will by a known male

inside. We arrived and also made repeated demands that the

complainant exit her home so that she could prove to us that

she was free to leave. She kept telling us that she would be

coming out the front door, then the back door, but she never

did. At one point she cracked open a door and we could see

that she was not injured. When asked, she said that there were

no guns in the house, and that the suspect in the home with her

was preventing her from leaving both verbally and physically.

He did this by inserting himself between her and any exit when

she tried to leave. The door then closed quickly.

Making sure that the rear door was watched by another

officer, I conferred with a Sergeant who agreed to my wanting

to make forced entry. After a few kicks, the front door flew

open and I was first to enter. Another officer discovered that

the suspect was with the complainant inside a locked rear

bathroom. The Sergeant and I alternated kicks to the bathroom

door. This door gave way and we rushed in to handcuff the

bewildered suspect who put up no resistance. He was arrested

for False Imprisonment (now called Unlawful Restraint) and for

some warrants.

A 6-year-old boy was with his 5-year-old brother and 3-year-

old sister, and a middle-aged woman of a different race inside a

Sam's Club Store. I was in uniform working there and was

surprised when I heard this little boy shout at the woman

"COME ON! COME ON!" Both little boys looked very angry and

impatient. The patient woman walked over to me and actually

had a smile on her face and asked me

"Officer, can you do something about him?" I told her that she

should feel free to give him a spanking; corporal punishment

was not illegal. She replied that she was a foster parent and the

state would not allow that. Understandably, it would become

far too easy for a foster parent to lose their patience with many

of these foster children, many of whom are quite frankly misfits,

or at least misunderstood. Short corrective swats on their

keister could easily become physical abuse from pent up anger.

Loud shouts of "COME ON! LET'S GO!" from a very angry little

boy to an adult was something I had never seen or heard

before.

    This foster Mom believed that kindness and patience and a

loving home were the keys to successful behavior modification.

    Three cars moving in the same direction approached a stop

sign single file. The first two cars stopped at the stop sign, but

the third car only stopped behind the second car. I made a

traffic stop on that last car. I had him hand me the open beer

can that was in his center console cupholder. Though he was

the sole person in the vehicle, the beer didn't belong to him. As

I was writing him a ticket for violation of open container law

while sitting in my police cruiser, his door opened. He

apparently had a question for me and started to step outside of

his car. His car began rolling forward because he never shifted

out of drive, and he was losing his balance and began to get tangled in his seat belt. As he lost his footing and was being pulled by his car, the thought occurred to me that because my emergency lights were activated, so was my video, and I might well record his death when he fell and was unable to regain control and got run over by his own vehicle. He was able to recover his balance and got back inside his car to put it in park.

He was from another country, and amusingly, his first name was "Duh".

A woman had been shoved and choked by her husband and then pushed out the front door. He was upset that she had been unable or unwilling to find work. We arrived to find that he had left the apartment, and the woman and her two girls already had a few loaded bags and suitcases, having arranged to go to a women's shelter. Deciding to help speed things along, I picked up a broken green garment bag to put into our police car, as we would be giving them transport. As I carried it, the contents partially spilled onto the stairwell. I put her treasured belongings back into her garment bag, and couldn't help but notice one item in a clear plastic bag that she apparently couldn't leave behind—a big rubber dildo. She had stooped to help me pick up the spilled items and knew that I saw it and flashed me an awkward smile.

Humorously, when we do a "civil standby" such as this, we always tell the person who is leaving to be quick and only take what they need and can't do without.

I was just 100 yards from a restaurant where I was going to meet a friend for lunch when a man ran out to the median waving his arms frantically to try to get my attention. He had just stopped his light brown van with "Linen Services Quality since 1929" in dark brown letters on the road along the curb to make a delivery. He left the engine running because he was only going to be gone a few minutes, but when he stepped back outside the van was gone. I quickly took the information for a stolen vehicle report, and sent out a "B.O.L.O. (Be-On-the-

Lookout) message to all police vehicles citywide. I completed my report after lunch and learned that an officer in south Dallas had spotted the vehicle and the suspect had been arrested.

We loved it when an opportunistic but unthinking crook stole a uniquely marked or colored vehicle because of their inability to blend in with traffic, sort of a subliminal "Here I am officer! Come and get me!" shout out to police in the area.

A woman phoned 911 because her boyfriend had told her mother that he was going to kill himself. She had just had an argument with her boyfriend the day before and told him that their relationship was over, and that she was leaving. He was distraught and went looking for his now ex-girlfriend at her mother's house. After he found out that she had gone to work, he told her mother "I might as well kill myself. I can't live without her." I drove to his address and saw his red truck in his driveway. I knocked on the front and back doors without any response. I phoned a Sergeant and appraised him of the circumstance and he agreed that a door should be forced open to assess the man's safety. Just as I took a step back to thrust a kick to hit the sweet spot, the other officer said to hold up. Walking from next door was the boyfriend; he had just been visiting with a neighbor. We walked into his house with him and let him get a cigarette and a cold drink to relax him. I explained the need to handcuff him when he finished to take him to a psychiatric hospital. He was reluctant at first, until I told him he could be handcuffed and taken to the county jail for resisting arrest, or he could cooperate and be released as soon as others determined that he wasn't in danger to himself and probably get medication to help him with his mood swings. He turned around and put his hands behind his back. I did a quick visual home sweep to make sure he didn't have anything obvious with which to hurt himself. I found a large kitchen knife lying in his bathtub. It was unbloodied but represented his suicide potential and was a fact that hospital personnel should know. I secured it.

A few U.S. Marshals and a Dallas Police Officer were working together to locate a homicide suspect on this Easter Sunday. The murder suspect had called from a Kroger pay phone and the call had been traced. About 10 minutes later, he phoned again from the same pay phone. Another officer and me waited nearby. When the U.S. Marshals arrived, the suspect had just entered his vehicle that was being watched in the parking lot. As he drove off, we were told to move in. The suspect drove into an apartment complex being followed by a U.S. Marshals vehicle, and two police cars. The obvious was stated over the radio when someone said "He will Run." I was the second police vehicle and when I turned right into the complex drive all vehicles were stopped and the suspect vehicle driver door was open. I never did see the suspect inside that complex, and he pulled the slip on all of us that day, possibly entering an unknown apartment. At least he lost his transportation which we had towed.

I was driving in the left lane of three lanes, and anybody turning onto my road had an empty right and middle lane. Sure enough (it happens to all drivers), a motorist turned into my lane instead of the other open lanes, forcing me to drastically reduce my speed. I made a traffic stop.

He ended up having a parole violation with a tagged warning "Violent tendencies," though he was subdued with no issues. He was going back to prison because of a driving error that got him noticed by the police. Had he simply pulled into one of the two open lanes, fate would not have intervened.

I stopped an older man for not wearing his seat belt. He had a "10X" hit, meaning that he was a known offender when I checked his ID on my computer. He was recently released from prison, having served 25 years for murder. I returned to his vehicle and told him that I could see that he served time in prison for murder, but that he had paid his debt to society and that I was going to give him a warning instead of a ticket. He

thanked me, then broke down and cried.

A 94-year-old woman fed her 100-year-old husband some ice

cream at 9 p.m. Sometime overnight before 8:30 a.m., he

passed away in his sleep. He had been a soldier just after WWI,

and had pictures of General "Blackjack" Pershing and General

Billy Mitchell on his wall, as well as old bi-plane pictures. He

was as skinny as skinny could be. At a century old, he still had a

sound mind, but not a sound body. He had died wearing a t-

shirt and an adult diaper.   For better or for worse, the blessed

couple had taken care of each other for over 75 years.

A lake user was bicycling down the trail in the surrounding

forest and called police to report having heard what he thought

might be a woman screaming from the woods. We arrived and

listened, but heard nothing. Someone suggested that it could

be the cry of a bobcat that can at times mistaken as the scream of a woman. We listened to an internet bobcat screech on a cellphone and concluded that was probably what he had heard.

At a crisscross of roads adjacent to an intersection of two freeways, another bicycle officer and I spoke to a young homeless woman soliciting from the median. She had been handled by police before for panhandling and prostitution. She said she had a female social worker that brought her food and checked up on her sometimes. The solicitor was polite, but dirty, and lived under a freeway bridge. It wasn't the best of accommodations for a woman who was 8 months pregnant, but there were no other homeless people anywhere around, and she was not far from some businesses and from motorists if she needed someone to call for an ambulance.

I thought about the health of the baby because I doubted she had been drug and alcohol free during her pregnancy.

Patrolling White Rock Lake, I saw 4 young children swimming. Swimming hadn't been legal in several decades, but there were occasionally some swimmers, almost always immigrants that didn't know swimming violated a long-standing city ordinance. These 4 kids included a girl of about 5 years old. They had adult supervision. What made the group noticeable was that all of these young children were naked. This was something that you don't see in a modern nation, but was probably common place in their country of Nepal. I supposed in a third world nation a young western child wearing a swimsuit would be perceived as unusual. A couple of men in a nearby pickup truck had been watching. We looked at each other and smiled, and the men shook their heads.

I had the kids get out of the water and informed their parents the best I could about no swimming being allowed.

A rookie of mine engaged in a conversation with a woman who noticed his last name was her last name too. Most strangely and distinctively, his and her mother each had the

same maiden name, and same first name, but his mom was

from Texas and hers was from California. Truly bizarre.

   Someone called the police after hearing a woman scream

from the woods. I arrived and as I walked that way, I heard a

blood-curdling scream. Fearing the worst, I "cleared leather"

with my pistol and trotted over to that general direction. I saw

three young men emerge from the woods with a young woman.

My first thought was that these men raped her, but--though

assisted--she was walking with them and fully clothed. The 18-

year-old girl was with her boyfriend and two of his friends, and

had reportedly used LSD and was having a "bad acid trip". The

boyfriend explained that she actually did drugs often, just never

the hallucinogen LSD. She had wanted to try it, so they thought

being outside with her and watching her reaction would help

keep her safe. The girl had unsteady balance and a frightened

look in her eyes, but in her altered mental state she still

recognized me as a police officer. I told her that I was there to help and that she was going to be okay, and she tightly grasped my hand with one of hers.

We walked toward the awaiting ambulance in the parking lot. She was eventually released. Amidst her boyfriend's objections, I took her to her nearby father's home despite the boyfriend telling me that he would take care of her. I brought the girl home to her dad and had the three young men wait several houses down to avoid any likely confrontation.

I wrote her a public intoxication ticket so at least she had a consequence for experimenting with a dangerous drug, and released her into dad's custody. Though he admitted that he didn't have the best relationship with his daughter, he was adamant that he knew that she didn't do drugs at home or when she was away at college.

If you don't have the best relationship with somebody, it probably stems from your not having spent enough time with them one on one.

On a 97-degree day, a fisherman had two empty beer bottles and four cold bottles with condensation on a six pack two feet away from him. He received an alcohol in the park ticket. He was alone, but claimed that the beer didn't belong to him.

I wrote a woman a ticket for running a red light, and subsequently another one for no insurance. In Spanish, I commented "No eseguranza. Firme aqui" (No insurance. Sign here). She signed the ticket "No eseguranza". I pointed out her mistake by saying "No, su nombre" (No, your name). She smiled embarrassingly and then signed her name.

The Fire Department had a call regarding a man who was slumped over his steering wheel at an intersection. The man was not in need of medical attention, he was just intoxicated. I happened to drive up on the situation. The man was unmistakably inebriated, and I asked him how much he had to drink. Instead of the usual "one" or "two" answer, he declared that he had not been drinking. I had him step out of the car and he automatically assumed the search position putting his hands against his car. I had to hold onto his arm to prevent him from falling and stumbling. Unable to complete the sobriety tests, I arrested him for DWI and placed in the police cruiser.

On the way to jail, I told him that he shouldn't be driving because he was obviously drunk and should've known it was dangerous to drive. He replied "I don't know. I'm fucking stupid I guess."

At the jail in the Intoxilyzer room, the arrestee showed serious unsteady balance, having to constantly use the wall to support himself when his balance wavered. Additionally, unprovoked and in a drunken stupor voice, he slowly said "Why don't you go ahead and beat the hell out of me and get it over with?"

He may not have remembered this drunken episode when he sobered up, but he would be aware of the consequences. He already had two misdemeanor DWI convictions on his criminal

record, so this third DWI arrest was a felony.

While waiting at the scene of a bank robbery with other

officers, a suspicious person call came out in the same large

shopping center about a man of the same race as our bank

robber, seen changing clothes outside in the parking lot of

another bank. I rushed over there and detained the male who I

saw had just finished putting some clothes into his duffel bag. I

needed to wait there a few more minutes until another officer

showed up with a bank teller witness from the other bank to

exclude him as the bank robber, which she eventually did after

their arrival.

Ironically, this suspicious person grew tired of waiting with

me and of all the things to possibly say, he asked "What'd I do?

Rob a bank or something?" He had just bought some local thrift

store clothes and was trying them on. Coincidentally, it was a blue shirt and blue pants, the same clothing worn by the real

bank robbery suspect.

At my Sam's Club job, I periodically checked the parking lot

and while out there would scan vehicles parked in handicapped

spaces to be sure they had a handicapped placard on their rear-

view mirror, or a handicapped license plate. One car that I

noticed had neither so I kept an eye on it for the eventual

return of the owner. A pretty teenaged girl stepped into the car

and I approached and asked her why she was parked in a

handicapped space. She said that her mom had just had knee

surgery and that she was going to drive over to the exit to pick

her up. I took her word for it, though I had my doubts. Sure

enough, the girl drove past the exit and kept on going, having

no ailing mother with her or anyone else.

I knew she had to be smiling, feeling good about herself, how

her quick thinking kept her from getting a ticket, and how she

was so smart and the police officer was so dumb and trusting. I ran the license plate registration and mailed a parking ticket to her address, not needing her name for a parking citation. I enclosed a note describing the girl, along with the date/time/place/circumstances. I had a call from the girl several days later, asking me to cancel the ticket, giving me a bogus cockamamie excuse. Of course, I refused. She was just some spoiled, pretty girl used to getting what she wanted, even if it involved deceiving the police.

I was in a parking lot typing up a report. It was common for someone to pull up alongside a police officer to report an accident, a crime, directions, etc. This time a man pulled up alongside of me and said "Hello Officer. How would you like a watermelon?" "Sure!" I said with a smile. He was heading home from having worked a farmer's market.

A woman bought several cans of compressed air for cleaning keyboards. Rather than use these cans for the expressed purpose, she inhaled perhaps three of these 10 oz. cans. She had looked like she was discombobulated, and eventually passed out. Some customers alerted loss prevention inside the store and they came out to investigate. Their persistent banging on her windows aroused her, and responding paramedics called us. The woman had been taking Effexor for depression, and likely just wanted to feel better by getting high on inhalants. She completely ignored the instructions on the can, as they defeated her purpose; "If inhaled, get fresh air immediately. Intentional inhalation of high concentration of vapor is harmful and may cause heart irregularities, unconsciousness, or death." She didn't want to go with the paramedics, so I gave her a choice: go with them voluntarily, or with us forcibly to the psych hospital. She went with them.

An apartment complex Assistant Manager wasn't seen at work one morning, but then someone remembered that he was supposed to be in another state, supposedly having just left that same morning.

A leasing agent--on loan from another property--was showing a prospective tenant a vacant apartment. They thought they smelled paint or something as they were touring the apartment. The door was opened that led to the garage, and the leasing agent immediately saw a section of vent duct wrapped around the right side of the car, with a section ending inside an open right backseat door window where it was duct-taped. The shocked leasing agent knew immediately what had happened, and hurried back to the office. A maintenance man rushed to the apartment, opened the overhead garage door and opened all four car doors, then felt for a pulse on the man sitting behind the wheel; there was no pulse. 911 was called. The man's car had been seen by the office at around 5 p.m. the previous day, where he probably had got a key to the vacant apartment. He was the Assistant Manager.

His suicide was pre-meditated. He had bought the vent duct

at the Home Depot, as the receipt was found in the car along

with the box. He had neatly duct-taped the other end of the

hose to an exhaust pipe, with enough gasoline in the fuel tank

to do the job, but not so much so that other apartment

residents were in danger of carbon monoxide asphyxiation

(other apartments were checked and all residents were fine).

The ignition switch was on, but the engine had stopped because

the fuel tank was empty. No note was found. The suicide

victim was obviously troubled by something, and the leasing

agent was certainly very troubled over finding him, especially on

her birthday.

Police were circling a neighborhood looking for bank robbers

and any evidence from it. I drove past an old man walking

down the sidewalk who seemed to have something in his hand.

The last indication was that the bank robbers had last been right

here in this area. I U-turned and drove slowly not far from the old man. The old man was now curious, and stopped to say

aloud "Are you looking for this officer?" as he opened his hand.

Indeed, I was. He had some of the evidence that we had been

looking for that he had casually picked up from the sidewalk,

thinking it to be an unusual trinket. It had been tossed away by

the bank robber as he fled.

I made a U-turn after I saw what I thought might be a fender-

bender in a parking lot. After completing my turn, I glimpsed

that one of two males sitting on a concrete bus stop bench had

thrown a crumpled-up piece of paper into the middle of the

road. From a distance, I saw his curious face looking my way

wondering if I had seen him do that. His question was

answered when I stopped in the right lane right in front of them

and turned on my emergency lights. After I stepped out, I

pointed at the litterer and asked if he had some ID. "No sir, we

are from India, we only have passports." Though I didn't ask his

friend for ID, they both gave me their passports. Asking them if they knew why I had stopped, they both said "Yes sir", and the

litterer added "I didn't see a dust bin anywhere." I informed

him that he could have walked to the McDonalds just 20 yards

behind them to throw away the paper, or he could have just put

it in his pocket until he arrived home. The litterer dashed out

and retrieved the piece of paper he had thrown onto the

roadway after he replied "Yes sir. You are right". I asked them if

they lived here, and I was told they are tourists. I inquired "Do

you like this country?" "Yes" was the reply from both. "Then

have some respect for this country". "Yes sir, thank you sir," as

I handed them their passports.

I was having my dinner inside the Dallas Police building at

the Texas State Fair one evening. A motorcycle officer brought

over two handcuffed brothers who looked to be in their thirties.

The motor Jock asked me to watch them while he searched for

a police detective. I heard the story of their arrest from these

brothers, who were intoxicated which explained their lack of good judgment. One brother had noticed an unattended police motorcycle and saw it as an opportunity to defy and defile authority and relieved himself upon it. The other drunken brother laughed and then walked over and stood shoulder-to-shoulder with him, both urinating all over it. They thought it was hilarious, until they turned around to see the motorcycle officer standing behind them. He had waited until they finished before he detained and escorted them to this holdover area.

I held the phone to one of their ears so that he could talk to his wife. It was a short conversation, telling his wife that he and his brother had been arrested at the State Fair for "doing something stupid. It seemed like a good idea at the time." He added that they shouldn't be in jail long because it was minor and she shouldn't worry, without ever having told her the specifics of their brain fart. Both happy drunks received citations for urinating in public and were taken to Detox.

____

Working as a bicycle officer at White Rock Lake, I detected the scent of burning marijuana, and jumped the parking lot curb onto the grass to ride over to two separate pairs of men. I couldn't discern which pair had the drug, so I guessed and rode over to the wrong couple of men. Though I was only ten yards away from the other two men, when I rode over to them one still had the marijuana blunt in his hand. He also went to jail for Failure to ID when he gave me a false name and DOB.

A horse rider foolishly decided to ride his horse over a railroad trestle bridge, with only gaps of air between the railroad ties. The horse didn't want to go and knew better, but the rider urged him forward. The horse quickly took a misstep, and the horse faltered when a rear leg slipped through the gap up to its elbow, quickly followed by one of its front legs doing the same when it panicked and struggled to stand. The man fell from the horse and nearly off the bridge, hanging on with one hand and dangling in the air until he pulled himself up again.

How can a horse see where it is placing its rear legs? Two legs

stuck in the railroad ties, the horse screamed in panic unable to

free itself. The man can offer no assistance given the weight of

the horse. The horse screamed often from fear, and what an

arriving Veterinarian determined to be two broken legs. The

guilt-ridden rider didn't even wait to get permission from the

owner and decided to have the Vet put the horse out of its

misery. A long needle was presented by the Vet for euthanasia.

This horse--intelligent as they are--sensed the somber mood

and instinctively tried to flee, but could only rock back and

forth. It cried and whinnied several times as the lethal injection

was administered. There was one final high-pitched loud, long

whinny from the horse, as the last breath of life passed from his

lungs, followed by the stillness of death. The rider couldn't bear

it and stood nearby with his head lowered and his hands held

tightly over his ears as tears streamed down his face.

____

I stepped inside a 7-11 to get a cup of coffee before I went to traffic court. As I walked inside, I noticed a car parked crookedly several spaces away. Someone told me that a woman was slouched over on the driver side and was possibly unconscious. She was just as the witness described. I opened the door expecting to find an intoxicated woman. She raised her head and began to speak slowly, but I smelled no alcohol. She informed me that although she had been driving a vehicle, she suffered from narcolepsy, a sleep disorder. She had felt a "sleep seizure" coming on and pulled over to take her medicine, and was waiting for it to metabolize in her system and cause alertness so that she could once again drive. I told the clerks inside and when I returned she was fully awake. Feeling fine, she drove away.

Later, I made a trip to the Department of Public Safety to see if she should be driving with that condition. I was told that if a Doctor signed something for her stating it was his belief that when properly treated she could drive safely, she could then have a driver license. Not knowing if that was the circumstance,

I completed a request form that would allow DPS to question

her about any current medical conditions.

I had just turned the corner to drive into a parking garage to

work my Sam's Club side job when I spotted a teenaged male

ahead of me. He finished drinking a juice and placed the empty

plastic juice container atop a yellow post, and continued

walking. I pulled alongside of him and leaned over toward my

now open passenger window so that he could see my police

uniform to erase any doubt he had about my identity. I told him

that he needed to go back and pick that up. "What?" he

replied. I re-phrased "You need to go back and pick up that

trash you left back there." This is where most everyone would

simply say "yes sir", comply, and then continue walking. Not

this kid. Playing dumb, he said "What?" again. I stepped out of

my personal car, and pointed over at his empty bottle, telling

him that he needed to go back and pick up his trash because he

was littering. Still not complying, he just said "Dude, why you
messing with me?" I asked him for his name and he was at first
reluctant to give it, wondering aloud why I needed it. I told him
by state law he was required to give me his name and birthday,
and that I was writing him a ticket. He gave me his name, but
not his birthday. He told me the school that he used to attend
before he dropped out last year. I raised my police radio from
its holder to ask for a cover squad so that I could use the
computer. Before I could say a word, he broke and ran. I
managed to react quick enough to grab an arm but his
momentum pulled him free. He nearly fell when he struck the
side of a fuel price sign, then regained his balance and hoofed it
uphill and he was gone. As a 52-year-old officer I wasn't going
to catch a lean 17-year-old runner, so I let him go without
broadcasting a description on the radio. His new ball cap fell off
of his head when he ran from me. I picked it up along with his
trash, and placed it under some garbage in a trash can 15 yards
away.

I went inside the store to work my shift and phoned our Youth Division to ascertain if my evader had been handled before by the police as I suspected.   His given name and former school were correct, so with that I retrieved his birthday. I was sent a picture of him to confirm that identity, and I filed on him at large for Evading Detention. He would have that warrant as well as a pre-existing warrant for Resisting Arrest the next time he was detained by police.

At an unknown time over a weekend, unknown suspects cut a padlock of a gate at a company truck yard. They entered with 4 tractor trailer cabs and stole four, 48-50 foot semitrailers that had almost 12,000 cases of oatmeal and syrup valued at over $400,000. The company had the trailer numbers recorded, but not the license plates for the trailers. This was undoubtedly many hours beyond the time of the crime, so it was a cold trail anyway and the trailers were out of state if not already in Mexico.

This was the largest theft report I'd had in my 10 years as an officer at that time, but I didn't depress them further by mentioning that. At least one person lost their job from the commission of this crime.

I did a traffic stop one night and the motorist didn't have any ID on him. He gave me his name and birthday, and I made a trip back to the cruiser for a computer subject check. The suspect showed a parole violation. I summoned an officer to cover me for safety, and I informed the motorist of his parole violation as well as ticket warrants. He didn't believe it, and he gave me his name and birthday again, and I told him that I had written it down correctly the first time. He stepped out of the car as instructed and was completely compliant as I handcuffed him. Because he didn't have identification he would have to be printed at the County jail anyways to confirm that he was who he claimed to be. As I was completing the Book-in and warrant only sheets, the arrestee informed me that he needed to tell me something. He was going to tell me the truth because I was a

nice officer. He continued that he had given me his brother's

name and date of birth because he knew that if he had given

me his true name and DOB that I would quickly ascertain that

he had a parole violation which he knew about. He damned

sure didn't think that his brother had a parole violation too! I

notified the dispatcher of the error so that there was time to

intercept the wrongly named teletype before the parole

violation for his brother was confirmed as valid, and started

confirmation on the correct parole violation warrant.

A drunk male had been wandering around a Motel 6 for

hours with his two dogs, and someone called the police. We

arrived, but he was back inside his room, so we couldn't arrest

him and left after we told him that he needed to stay in his

room until he sobered up. We departed. Twenty minutes later

someone called about him again. This time we arrested him for

Public Intoxication, and his two dogs were put in protective custody by Animal Control. Despite being a staggering drunk, in his mind we arrested him for no reason. According to him he was just out walking around minding his own business.

I was working at a Sam's Club and standing by the exit door when from a distance of 10 yards a little 4 year old girl saw me as she was walking with her mother. She beamed a big grin, and then ran over to me at full speed with such force that she knocked me off balance as she hugged me around my thighs. I didn't know her; the mother explained that she just loved police officers.

Texas used to have a ridiculous, illogical legal condition called "Double Jeopardy" that applied to DWI arrests. If a motorist was arrested for Driving While Intoxicated and let's say had no driver license and was witnessed by the officer running a red light, the officer couldn't charge him with the traffic violations, only the DWI. This eventually changed. Common sense prevailed and police officers could charge them with the DWI

and for the traffic infractions.

A woman called about her son having found a body part in a

mostly dry creek bed in a small park. She said we could call if

we had any questions, so I doubted it was human otherwise she

would have remained. Curiously, the body parts were two

horse hooves with about a foot of leg still attached to each,

found about 20 yards apart. They had been cut off cleanly with

some kind of saw, still fresh with no smell of decomposition and

the joint above the hooves was still flexible. As a long shot, I

called to make sure no detective had a horse theft offense, and

then put the hooves in a covered trash can to make sure no one

else called about them. No other horse carcass parts were

found.

I thought the wording on a call was incorrect, so I called the

Reporting Person who assured me that it was correct and that no mistake was made. A woman had been walking her German

Shepherd at the lake and had squatted and defecated on a

vehicle. I found her plop on a vehicle running board and

thought maybe she meant to do it between two vehicles and

missed. Then I realized that she had left a deposit on two other

vehicles as well. It remained an unsolved mystery because she

was not found.

An ex-con spoke to us about just wanting to leave a woman's

apartment. He had been staying there the last 4 months, and

feared that because there may be arguing that she would claim

that he struck her, and that the simple allegation whether true

or not would send him back to jail and result in a probation

violation.

We took him back to their apartment after a pat down and he

began to gather his clothes under our watchful eyes while she

also watched. She surprised us when she loosely carried out a

BB gun, always startling until we ascertained that it wasn't real.

She told us it belonged to him. I told him that as an ex-con he

had no business being around any gun, even a BB gun because it

resembled the real thing. The embarrassed ex-con said that he

got off the bus one day and found it in the bushes (sure you did

bud), but he didn't want it anyway.

After he walked out with a few bags of his clothes and

departed, she told us that her now ex-boyfriend had boasted of

having "Jacked" some people and mentioned the locations

when he told her the two stories of his robberies. I made sure

that she was not just being vindictive and she swore to me that

he had told her about them. I got the details and contacted the

adjacent suburb where the alleged offenses occurred to give

them some info and my incident report number.

I put the unwanted BB gun in our property room as Found

Property with my linked report.

I went to a house as a favor to the Oklahoma Highway Patrol.

I was to contact the woman there and have her call them

because there had been a serious accident. That was all that I could tell her. A male trucker had got into an accident and was killed, possibly from having fallen asleep at the wheel. The woman was believed to be his mother-in-law, whose name and address was found in his wallet.

Our first call one morning was about a man who had written a check from his closed account. We arrived to discover that he had been in Houston for a month and may not have known that the bank closed his account for all check writing after he told them that one checkbook had been stolen. He was also waiting 15 minutes at the grocery store where he had tried to use his check until we arrived, and wasn't at all nervous. In short order this very effeminate and polite man began to share highlights of his trip with us. He had gone to Houston to attend an event called "SPLASH!", which was a huge gay beach party. He also went there to get silicone injections in his chest. Wearing blue fingernail and toenail polish, he encouraged us to call his roommate, because she would be home. "What's her name?" I asked. "Oh, he's really a guy. I call him lover or girlfriend." The LGBTQ community is label intensive and confusing at times.

I stopped a man for speeding 65 in a 45 zone. He said "officer, I'll be honest with you. I was in a hurry to get to Presbyterian Hospital to see my mother who is very ill. Can't you just give me a break?"

"65 in a 45. That's kind of hard to overlook."

"Please? Officer, I have a good driving record, you can check. I won't do it again." I told him I'd be right back and walked to my car to write him a speeding ticket. As I was writing, he got out of his truck and walked back to me, thereby using more of his supposedly precious time and said "I demand to see your odometer!" Now I knew he meant his clocked radar speed but I decided to play along. I pointed through my steering wheel to my odometer and said "Here it is". A look of disgust and frustration washed over his face.

"I demand to see my odometer!"

"I don't have it".

"Why not? I demand to see my odometer! I know my rights!"

"I don't have it".

"Why not? Where is it?"

 It's up there in your truck".

 He once again wore befuddlement all over his face. He finally said that he wanted to see the speed that he was driving.

"Why didn't you say so. I don't have it."

"I know my rights, you have to show that to me. That's the law!"

"No. I'm not required to show you your speed. Whoever told you that I have to show you your clocked radar speed was mistaken. I'm not required to show you anything".

"I have an attorney! I'll see you in court!"

 "That's your prerogative."

An ex-boyfriend wanted to get back together with a woman. He tracked her down and tried knocking on the door. She didn't answer, hoping that he would go away. He located a broken out open window and brazenly crawled inside, then found her upstairs lying on her bed. He screamed at her "Where you been hiding bitch! I couldn't find you. You can't hide from me you fucking bitch!" (He needed some work on his pickup lines and ability to woo women). He yanked her by the ankles and pulled her off the bed onto the floor, then kicked her on her back and legs a few times. He got on top of her and straddled her with his knees and tried to strike her in the face, but she shielded his blows with her hands over her face. She squirmed loose and ran across the street to a pay phone to call the police. He followed her after first grabbing a soda from the fridge. He caught up to her and poured the remainder of his soda over her head, with the admonition that she would never amount to anything without him (ironically from a guy who was just released from jail two weeks earlier after a seven month stay).

We had a call to Doctors Hospital regarding an unruly patient. An overweight male in his 50's was sitting calmly on a bed in an E.R. room. He had been there before and was despondent, living out of his car, but only had the potential for violence according to them; he hadn't done anything yet. We were told that despite being overweight he was HIV positive for 10 years and had "full-blown" AIDS. He had told them that he didn't want to be here anymore. The hospital couldn't release him to go to a psychiatric facility until he was cleared medically, as he had ingested an unknown number of pills. The hospital hadn't expected us to arrive so fast, making the call to 911 thinking it would take a while for us to respond and by that time he would be ready for transport. I decided that we weren't going to wait, and notified the hospital security staff to keep an eye on him until they were ready to have the police take him to a psych hospital.

Hours later, we heard on the radio that some officers were going to the hospital for the same patient. We could not return because we were en route to Narcotics for a drug house raid briefing, luckily for us. The patient had broken a disposable razor that he had and pulled out the razor blade, then sliced his throat and arms. We'd been told that it was a bloody HIV mess, and the medical staff was understandably cautious about helping him until they were certain that he was no longer a danger. The responding officers managed to render him weaponless, and he was tied to the metal arm guards of a portable bed so the staff could stitch up his self-inflicted wounds without his interference.

A couple was staying with a tenant, and the male of the couple decided one morning to turn down the thermostat because he was too warm. The tenant felt a chill after a while and discovered that someone had changed the thermostat, and an argument ensued. The two men began fighting, mostly wrestling over this petty reason. The woman tried to be a peacemaker and intervened verbally, but was choked by the tenant for her good intentions. She was saved by her boyfriend who pulled the tenant off her. When I arrived with the other officer all was calm. I did a routine radio subject check and determined with the aid of the tenant's social security number that he had been an out-of-state fugitive for 1 ½ years. Du Page County, Illinois, wanted him for Aggravated Battery. The tenant was surprised but cooperative and was arrested without incident.

Two officers would be sent from 900 miles away to extradite him back from the Dallas County Jail.

An auto parts store customer noticed a woman pull into a handicapped parking space and decided to confront her because he didn't see a blue handicapped placard on her rear-view mirror, nor a handicapped license plate. Infuriated, he stormed over to her (not realizing that she had recent knee surgery) and barked "Lady! What the hell are you doing parking in the handicapped spot? You bitch! You don't have a handicapped sticker!" Words were exchanged after his incendiary remark. The woman's 11-year-old son stepped between his mom and this man, seemingly to protect her. The man reacted to "Leave my mom alone!" by easily shoving the boy to the ground, then went back to his car and drove away.

Unfortunately for him, an employee in the store overheard and witnessed the ordeal, and happened to be neighbors with the suspect. We showed up at the suspect's house, and he was surprised that we found him. He had not caused the boy any injury and received an assault citation.

A slim young blond woman was an occasional marathoner and practiced and stayed running fit by jogging the 9 mile radius of White River Lake. She was nearly finished with her run when she felt a hard tug on her ponytail from behind. Not waiting or wanting to see what might happen next, she took the initiative against this unknown male suspect and spun around to deliver multiple rapid punches to the man's face. Any thought that the suspect may have had about his being the aggressor and the female victim being a demure shrinking violet ended quickly. He ran off, undoubtedly shocked at the sudden role reversal, his unknown scheme having been foiled. The complainant told me that she had taken self defense classes. I suggested that if she was going to run late and finish near sunset that she should run in the other direction to finish in the open rather than in a darkened, wooded area.

I waited the next night in the hopes that I would encounter the suspect bent on revenge, but he never bothered anyone out there again.

A friend from a different patrol division would meet me for lunch once or twice a week for years. We had just finished when an undercover officer from his patrol division stated on his radio that a stolen vehicle had just become occupied, and we happened to be the closest patrol officers for the takedown. Miles down the freeway, about five other patrol cars caught up to us and both the male driver and female passenger were arrested at gunpoint.

The male arrestee said that his girlfriend—the other arrestee—was a topless dancer and that one of her customers had loaned her the vehicle. Apparently, it hadn't been quite like that, as it was confirmed as stolen. The male went to jail for UUMV, and the woman went to jail for a theft warrant and probation violation warrant. The woman also had a heroin kit, but no actual heroin. She admitted to just having done heroin a day earlier despite being three months pregnant.

She had a more difficult life than most people; she had been a foster child and mentioned that both her older foster brother and foster father had sexually abused her.

After 17 years in patrol answering 911 calls, I started working as a bicycle officer at White Rock Lake Park. Like Motorcycle officers, when I stopped someone for a violation I would only sometimes do a radio subject check for warrants. One Sunday, I dismounted my bicycle and walked around some cars in a parking lot and discreetly approached a large extended family at a picnic table. A couple of males saw me coming and quickly dumped the beer from their plastic cups, knowing that alcohol in the park was a city ordinance violation. For some reason, I overlooked them and just randomly focused my attention on a male who was walking away slowly, talking on his cell phone. He also had a cup in his hand which I correctly assumed was beer. He had no ID on his person, and so he verbally gave me his name and DOB, and I stepped a short distance away to check for a valid ID on my computer in the cruiser, which happened to be in the same parking lot. As I did this, I could see and hear his wife speaking to him, wondering why he gave me his correct information and asking why he didn't just lie to me. I could see his reaction of disgust as he told her still within my earshot that he was tired of running and that he just wanted to get it over with. I soon ascertained what he meant when I found and confirmed two felony warrants, one for aggravated assault with a deadly weapon, and the other for possession of marijuana more than 5 pounds.

The warrants were two years old. He was arrested peacefully.

I was a young rookie still in training when a police chase began elsewhere in my patrol division. My FTO had me drive to a gas station parking lot next to a SB entrance ramp to a freeway. The suspect vehicle and chase elements involved were SB on the Freeway, and would soon be upon us. I was about to join my first high-speed police chase! As they were fast approaching, I began to drive out of the parking lot to position myself closer. My Field Training Officer told me to stop, and asked me what I was doing. I told him I was about to enter the chase. He crushed my enthusiasm when he told me that he just

wanted to show it to me as the chase passed by us.

He was my least favorite trainer.

While on a bicycle I responded to a call involving security

holding a drunk male at a grocery store. When I arrived, the

suspect was already lying face down on the pavement with

three men holding him. I handcuffed him, and kept him down

with my right foot while I awaited for a cover unit in a police

cruiser. The drunk wiggled and squirmed but he couldn't get

up, mainly because his head and chest were hanging over a

curb. When the officer in a car arrived, we hoisted this big 220-

pound drunk to his feet. He had a foul mouth and didn't hold

back what he thought of me. Enroute to Detox (I drove), I had

just said a few non-inflammatory things to the drunken male,

but whenever I opened my mouth, he would kick the back of my

seat several times, so I decided to keep quiet and let my partner

do the talking.

The drunk --who was American Indian--identified with my partner who was black, saying that he "Understood prejudice and racism." He didn't see the irony and hypocrisy of sometimes laughing during his mostly one-sided conversation with my partner by calling him a black mother f and a mother f N several times. I could see that my partner was rattled and agitated, but did his best to ignore the profane racist slander.

When it came to allegations of racist police officers, citizens should realize that they are more prevalent on some police departments than on others. I never felt that the Dallas Police Department had a racist reputation within the minority community. There will be times when we stop the wrong person when searching for a suspect that fits your build and clothing descriptions, or has the same make and color of vehicle. But in my whole career of 26 years I can remember only one incident that I felt involved racism.

An older white male officer asked for a cover element on a traffic stop. I was close so I volunteered and arrived soon thereafter. The officer asked me to watch the young black male driver while he searched his vehicle. The black motorist asked me why the officer was searching his car. I candidly told him that I didn't know, I was just nearby and doing an officer a courtesy for officer safety. The motorist was upset at the situation because he didn't even know why he had been stopped and now the officer was searching his vehicle. Again, I told him that I was just there to watch him while the officer did a vehicle search, adding he would have to ask the officer the reason for the traffic stop when he was finished. Well, the officer finished he search and found no contraband. The motorist politely asked the officer the reason for the traffic stop, and the reason for the search, addressing the officer as "officer" and "sir". The officer ignored his requests and told me "We're done here Ray. Thanks for the cover," then entered his patrol car and drove away. I felt awkward, standing there with the motorist, who voiced that this wasn't right, that he couldn't believe what just happened. I agreed that the officer should have given him a reason for the stop, apologized that he didn't, and that I didn't know the reason.

If there was probable cause, the motorist should have been told because I guarantee that to this day, he believes there was no reason other than racism. I had thousands of traffic stops during my career and all knew why they were stopped, even if it was a case of mistaken Identity when looking for a suspect in a similar vehicle. I was always cognizant that I was more than just a name tag, that by being uniformed my comments and actions reflected on the reputation of the Dallas Police Department.

A couple had just moved into a complex two weeks before with their 3-year-old daughter. Rather than confront a downstairs neighbor about his thumping loud bass music pulsating through their floor, they opted to stomp on his ceiling to get his attention and signal that the music was too loud. The suspect received the message loud and clear, and ran up the stairs to bang on their door. When they opened it, the suspect

yelled and cursed at them, telling them that he's been living

there for 3 years and no white folks were going to tell him to

turn his music down. He also said that he had three 45's and he

might just shoot through his ceiling. They phoned police after

that threatening comment.

 We arrived to the complex and immediately heard the loud

music. The couple's 3-year-old girl had started crying when the

suspect had come to their door and shouted at her parents, and

she was still crying. My partner and I went to the suspect's

apartment and the music was still blaring, but he turned it down

when we asked him to do so. He presented an unofficial

Kentucky ID card, which we later verified as his true name at the

complex office on our way out. I wrote a ticket for disorderly

conduct for loud music. When told he needed to keep his music

turned down to avoid disturbing the peace, he angrily reiterated

that he's been here for 3 years and no white folks who have

only been here for two weeks are going to tell him what to do and turn down his music. His insolence continued when the other officer spoke with a southern drawl and the suspect openly mocked him for a bit by mimicking his speech. When his inquiry about how long he might be in jail if he didn't pay the ticket, he was told a day or two. He loudly pretended to laugh for about 15 seconds. After he received his ticket copies, the suspect demanded "Now get out!" We were done and left. Minutes later another loud music call came out from the same apartment. We returned and were told by the complainant that the suspect had just left in his vehicle, having made some gang gesture and promised "I'll be back mother-fuckers!"

A road was three lanes in each direction. I observed a car stopped in the right lane with his flashers on, so I stopped behind him after I turned on my emergency lights to ascertain the problem. He told me that his baby in the back seat had wiggled his way out of the car seat, and he was just putting him back in it. I told him a parking lot would've been safer.

"Isn't that what the hazards are for?"

"You're blocking a lane of traffic with a speed limit of 40 miles an hour. A parking lot or side street would've been safer."

He obviously didn't like being corrected and shot me a glare like I was the idiot, as he completed the harness buckling and then drove away.

A woman presented her ID card with a $2500.00 check at a bank. A check of the account showed that it had been frozen due to some checks having been stolen in a burglary. The woman was told there was a technical problem and if she'd like she could wait just a few minutes in the lobby. The woman (we found out) had been awake most of two days and was actually sleeping on the soft plush chair when we arrived a short time later. Her accomplice had been waiting in a car but then left after we arrived (we had no mention of another suspect or a vehicle). The groggy woman had a TX Department of

Corrections ID Card, and should've known better. She had two

felony convictions and at that time if this felony forgery resulted

in a conviction, she was to be sentenced to life in prison from

the "Three strikes and you're out" policy that was then state

law in Texas.

A woman went to an apartment because her brother-in-law

owed her $10. Her sister convinced her to leave by telling her

that he wasn't home. She left, albeit briefly. When she

returned, she tossed a 5 lb. stone through the bedroom

window, and heaved another large stone through a living room

window. When I arrived, she was wearing a crown of thorns

that she had made for herself, and kept repeating "In the name

of Jesus" or "In the blood of Jesus" at the beginning of every

sentence in our conversation. She had a long shard of broken

glass in her hand, as in stuck inside. I told her that she had a

choice today, that she could go to a hospital where people

would help her, or she could go to jail where people might hurt her. At first, she said that she wouldn't let us handcuff her, so I requested another officer for backup. She was a large woman and had several relatives present that could rally to her defense if she resisted or if they thought we were being too forceful when putting her hands behind her back. I again told her that she could have the power of making her own choice, and asked where she wanted to go. She put her hands behind her back and said that she wanted to go to a hospital.

They always made that choice, and if they didn't, we were going there anyway.

I was riding a bicycle on the north trail when I overtook a man on roller blades who was wearing an I-phone headset for music. As I passed him on his left, he simultaneously turned his head and spit to his left, spattering me with spit spray. I stopped my bicycle and he caught up, apologizing profusely. He said he didn't hear too well from his left side having had a gunshot go off next to his ear, so I scolded him louder.

Common sense should dictate that if you're on the right side of

a bicycle trail with woods on the right and you needed to spit,

you'd spit to your right and not to your left.

Paramedics had a call about a man down. They were waiting

for us with a man that had imbibed almost a ½ gallon of vodka,

but according to them was in no danger of alcohol poisoning.

He was semi-conscious but mostly slept. I couldn't get him to

do more than turn his head and stare at me blankly. I had

another officer come to the scene to help me put the drunken

sot into my car. We each had to put one of his arms over our

shoulders, and his feet dragged the whole way. His limp body

felt like all of his 190 lbs. He was unconscious, so we couldn't sit

him up to seatbelt him. I went to the other side and lifted and

pulled him across the seat while the other officer lifted and

pushed, and he now was sprawled over the entire back seat. He

was not seat belted, so we violated department policy by doing

this, but it was just one exception.

Making our way to Detox, I was busy talking and almost missed our turn. I quickly turned into a left turn lane. Well, now a vehicle in front of me that probably would have gone through the yellow light decided to stop and hit his brakes since there was a police car behind him. I hit my brakes, causing our prisoner to fly off the rear seat, hit the back of our seats, then fall to the floor where he was wedged. We laughed. I asked my partner to make sure that he could still breathe. His face was smooshed and contorted against the back of my seat, so we stopped in a parking lot and placed him back on the rear seat, still asleep. We brought him inside Detox on a wheelchair with someone pulling the wheelchair up the ramp backwards while my partner and I each pushed a foot from one of the prisoner's extended legs. We had never had a Public Intoxication arrest that was so drunk before.

An 18-year-old didn't come into work one morning to work her bank teller job. Her boss couldn't reach her by phone so drove to her apartment, but she didn't come to the door. He

called her mother, the emergency contact, who arrived from 40

miles away. Still no answer, so Mom called the police. I arrived

and went to the complex office for a key to do a welfare check,

but upon returning discovered that the interior deadbolt had

been slid over. Suicide? I could see that Mom was increasingly

nervous. She informed me that as she pulled up, she saw an

unfamiliar man leave her daughter's apartment and depart in a

red car. She said her daughter lived there alone. I located a

maintenance man and had him remove a window so I could

crawl through it (the metal door was too sturdy for a swift kick).

Entering, I announced "Dallas Police", and went to the bedroom

bathroom where I heard running water. I knocked, still thinking

that the girl may have committed suicide in the shower. I was

surprised to hear "Who is it?" I retorted "Dallas Police!" and

told her that she needed to come out. While I waited, I noticed

that next to me on a night stand next to her bed were two clear

sandwich baggies with some marijuana in them. At that

moment, she stepped out fully clothed, then looked at me, and looked back at the marijuana. And looked at me, then looked at the marijuana. It was too late, and I handcuffed her and brought her to the car.

The man that had left her apartment lived there, which Mom didn't know, nor did management who mentioned that it was a violation of her lease. The girl didn't want to talk to her Mom because they had a phone argument the night before.

All of this commotion and her subsequent arrest could've been avoided had the girl simply called her boss to tell him that she couldn't make it to work because of a migraine headache.

A woman who must have been an addict and was no rocket scientist presented a prescription at a pharmacy. The prescription drew attention from the Pharmacy Tech. The desperate moronic woman had crossed off the Doctor's phone number on the prescription with a pen and wrote down another phone number which was invalid (her own that was disconnected?). She went to jail for Forgery of a Prescription when the Doctor was contacted and stated that he had a

prescription pad stolen.

From the sound of things, the same woman had presented

the same prescription the previous day in a Dallas suburb but

was smart enough to walk away then. A detective could still file

that case on her if there was store video proof and if someone

in the pharmacy remembered her presenting the prescription.

A man's pickup truck was rear-ended by a woman on a slow

moving freeway, so they decided to take an exit and stopped in

a credit union parking lot to exchange info. The woman

appeared to have been drinking and asked the man if he could

not involve the police. The man told her that he had to phone

the police, and when he did, she just left her jalopy of a car and

ran off, staggering all the way. A witness had overheard part of

the conversation and thought it was a domestic, until the man

told him that the woman was a Hit & Run suspect, so he

followed her from his vehicle. I arrived and found several empty Budweiser beer bottles in her car.

The woman had only ran one street over and disappeared behind the high white fence of a house. My partner and I went to the house but no one answered the door. We walked into the back yard and expected a junk yard dog to come charging at us, as the yard was loaded with refuse tires, discarded appliances, and two unused cars. I happened to peer over the fence of the adjacent house. There was no trash in that backyard, but there were NINE junked cars.

We didn't find our Hit & Run suspect, but her vehicle was towed to our auto pound. We did the Hit/Run accident report as well as a Code Enforcement referral for the two addresses with the excessive backyard junk.

When you look around you don't see too many vanity plates, which made this incident even more of a coincidence. I typed a Texas vanity plate on my computer, and the uncommon name returned as a stolen vehicle...but from a Virginia license plate. The Texas vehicle vanity license plate with the same name had no issues.

On Christmas Eve, a woman's house was burglarized while she was visiting with neighbors. All of her wrapped gifts had been stolen as had her purse with all of her ID, credit cards, and money. She was leaving in the morning on Christmas Day to drive out of town for a trip that would take hours to go visit family but now had no presents for anyone, no way to buy any, no credit cards for gas, no cash, no ATM cards, and no banks were open. She started to cry and wondered what she would do.

Fate played a role this day. I had cashed a check the day before and had $200 in my wallet, but I wasn't going anywhere for Christmas because I had to work. She still had a check book in her house. I gave her my cash and just had her write me a personal check. She now had tears of joy that trickled down her face and she hugged me, telling me that I had saved her

Christmas.

An insecure man saw a picture of his girlfriend with another

man and illogically assumed that she must have been having sex

with him, which started an argument. The man grabbed the

woman from behind with both of his hands, placing them

around her neck and pulled her down to the floor. Next, he

straddled her and choked her briefly from the front as he was

atop her.

The fight ended, and the woman called the police. We

separated the man and woman to get truthful stories so no one

felt intimidated by the other's presence. The male was nervous

and walking around too much, so I told him to have a seat on

the couch. He ignored me, so after a couple more attempts to

convince him to sit on the couch I took him by the arm and

shoved him onto the couch because his being so unsettled

made me nervous. He kept looking over his right shoulder into an adjacent room as I stood a few feet in front of him. Twice he urgently tried to stand up, and twice I impeded his attempts and shoved him back down on the couch. After the elements of the offense were determined, I handcuffed him. When I asked him his name, he gave the wrong last name which was soon corrected by the girlfriend he had assaulted. Upset, he queried of her "What did you go and do that for?"

In the squad car just before we left for jail, he told me that he wanted to get off that couch to go into the other room because that was where he had his 12-gauge shotgun. He was charged with Assault and Failure to ID as a Fugitive because he had a warrant for UCW (Unlawfully Carrying a Weapon).

I was on the second floor of an apartment building looking for the apartment on my call sheet. I noticed a woman down in the parking lot below looking up at me, and she decided to speak. I correctly assumed that she had a mental issue.

"Officer! Officer! I'm worried! I'm sorry! He made me so

nervous that I wet my pants! See?" Then she spun around to

show me the wet vertical line in the middle of her pant seat. I

laughed to myself. The boyfriend shouted up to me moments

later that his bi-polar schizophrenic girlfriend was driving him

crazy. Sometimes she would chase him, wanting love and

affection, and other times she would tell him to get away from

her and then he would leave.

For training purposes, I volunteered me and my rookie for a

sexual assault call, as he had never had one in his 17 weeks of

training with his other trainers. The victim spoke little English

and required a Spanish speaker, though she had lived in the USA

for twenty-two years. She had been dating her boyfriend for

two years and broke up with him just three days earlier, last

having sex with him eight days earlier. They were currently just

friends. She and a female friend went with him to a party. Her

ex-boyfriend drank too much alcohol and was too drunk to

drive, so she let him and her friend sleep the night in her

apartment. During the night, her ex had sex with her against her will. Given the situation, she deliberated for several hours before she decided to involve the police after he left. We took her to the hospital for treatment and rape kit evidence. When we returned close to quitting time near midnight to drop her off at her apartment, a man approached her from the darkness to talk to her as she went to her door. Alarmed, we rushed over to intercept the intruder, suspicious of his late-night contact and intentions. It was her ex-boyfriend trying to engage her in a dalliance but she wanted no part of it or him. We arrested him and took him to jail.

Mid-afternoon in mid-July, I received a call about loud music coming from a car in a complex parking lot. As I entered the complex with my windows down, I could hear loud bass music and traced it to the vehicle listed on the call. The driver door was open, and the owner was on his back seat working on his car. I informed him about the loud music complaint and he turned it off. I obtained his verbal name and DOB, and he added that he knew that he had some ticket warrants. When I asked how many, he replied "A bunch." I said that I wasn't going to overlook a bunch of tickets. The man said that he had his ID and some papers inside his apartment, and that he could go get them. I told him to shut off his ignition, roll up the windows, lock the car, go upstairs to his apartment and wipe the sweat off his face, put on some clothes (he only had on a pair of gym shorts), then return. I reminded him that he was being lawfully

detained and he needed to return ASAP. The suspect walked to his apartment which I could see and went inside. I saw that the suspect had a valid DL on the computer. After ten minutes, the suspect had not returned so I went to his apartment door just forty yards away. After a few minutes of knocking and ringing his doorbell, there was no answer though I could hear a TV. He thought his scheme would prevent him from going to jail. It did, temporarily. His car- which I would have left in the parking lot--

was now towed, and I did an at-large offense of Evading

Detention. The complex office was still open to verify his

identity, and a maintenance man had seen him earlier working

on his car.

Humorously, he didn't have any unpaid ticket warrants for his

arrest. Apparently not enough time had passed for them to

become warrants. He had made a false presumption, but now

the criminal charge that I had initiated would soon be processed

and become a misdemeanor warrant for his arrest.

If you as the driver are being polite to an officer that stopped

you, but your passenger is a completely disrespectful jerk,

you're probably getting a ticket. For example, I don't want to

hear loud demands of "Take a hike!" once much less three

times during a traffic stop.

I had my windows down sitting in my squad car typing up a report when I heard what sounded like a little girl screaming "HELP! Somebody help me! Waaaaah! Help Me!"

 I turned my head to see a girl of about twelve run around the corner of a house, then run across her front yard. Hearing her panicked, shrill screams, I thought she was in imminent danger or needed help for someone else. Then I saw that she wasn't running from but going after her two dogs that had escaped from an open gate in her back yard. I stepped out of the car to help, as she was just across the residential street from me. The girl chased after the small dog that had ran into another fenced yard while I squatted down on the sidewalk to coax the larger brown dog to come towards me. He was slowly wagging his tail and seemed friendly. The dog came to me and I was petting him. The girl had captured the small dog and I told her to go home and get a leash for this larger dog. To lightly hold this dog, I placed one hand loosely on his neck as I stroked his fur with the other. While I was crouching and he was sitting, he jerked to leave the spot but I held him back. I talked in a low

voice and whispered to the dog, and briefly looked him in the

eyes. As if sensing my lecture about his being a bad dog, he

lunged himself toward my face and punched me on my nose

with his snoot. Having hurled his weight for the nose punch, he

walked away when I let go and I stood up to make sure the

painful poke didn't involve any canine teeth; I was lucky, I still

had a nose, and it wasn't bleeding.

The girl returned with her mother and retrieved the bigger

dog.

A woman had successfully completed drug rehab and was no

longer a meth user. She was wondering and worried about how

her meth-using ex-boyfriend was doing, so she called to offer

help and they talked for a while.

After 3 A.M. one morning, he called her needing a ride home

because he just did some meth (he had no car, no job, and at 38

lived with Mom). She knew that she couldn't be around the

drug or people on the drug if she was to stay clean and sober, so she told him that she couldn't give him a ride and be an enabler. He was angry and texted her "If I ever see you again bitch, I swear to God I will kill you fucking whore!"

I made a harassment report for her, and gave his info to an officer friend who worked in our Deployment section. The suspect wasn't currently at home but they wanted to wait for him to return in order to arrest him for his Dangerous Drugs warrant.

The primary entrance into a small neighborhood was like a catch basin for rainwater running downhill from two sides of the outside street. Drainage can only be adequate if rainwater has a place to flow. Torrential rains one day led to this neighborhood being in two to three feet of water, and it was flooding into people's flood plain homes.

I went to an Army Reserve Center next to our NE Patrol Division and spoke to a Commanding Officer about borrowing a

Humvee, which rode much higher above the road to allow me to do some water rescue work. He assigned me a driver, and we entered the flooded area with me using the speaker to find people who needed help. One man flagged us down about his very old mother whom we rescued in a few feet of high water inside her house, and we took them to a nearby friend's house outside the rain deluged area.

The rain subsided a short time later and the rain-swollen waters began to recede.

A man had just been given an expensive gold chain by a friend, and had placed it on the porch chair that he was sitting on to go inside. The suspect that was sitting beside him entered the house moments later and went into the bathroom. Minutes later, the gold chain was found to be missing and the suspect was asked if she had taken it. She was coughing but denied it and replied that they could search her if they didn't believe her.

She had no pockets on her clothing, and then—still coughing--

said that she needed to go home.

I listed her as a suspect, but if she denied having swallowed

the chain and if she didn't blab about her action, there was

nothing that could be done about the common unremarkable

gold chain even if the complainant did see it again hanging

around her neck.

I was training a rookie when we both noticed two cars parked

in the right lane using their emergency flashers. We circled

around to see if we could help them, assuming that a minor

accident had just happened. As we U-turned, both vehicles

began to pull away. They must have completed exchanging

info, but I told my rookie to follow the vehicle dragging his rear

bumper as he pulled into a rail station parking lot, thinking that

we could offer him a ride home. The 60-year-old man stopped,

and we stopped behind him. Suddenly, the motorist had his

backup lights on and seconds later he backed into us. I turned on our emergency lights knowing that the video backed up thirty seconds to record when I did. Upon hitting us, the man drove away, probably just because he knew he had hit something. He stopped about fifty yards from the accident scene after I activated our air horn and police siren. I approached his vehicle and smelled some alcohol, but it was not overpowering. He explained that he had some wine with his lunch hours before. He was just out doing his wife (who had an incapacitated hip) a favor by bringing her some takeout dinner.

I called an Accident Investigator and a supervisor, and then did some sobriety testing as did another officer a bit later. We completed writing out our accident statements and a needed form for city owned vehicles.

The male driver that caused the backing accident had a PBT (Portable Breath Tester) reading of .13, well over the minimum of .08 required for a DWI. Our drunk driver couldn't blow hard enough to give a sample of his breath at the county jail and so agreed to a blood draw. I hadn't done a DWI report in a few years and some things had changed. A young and understanding sergeant was kind enough to make a few report corrections.

Back at the station I completed a video tag request form so that my video evidence would get downloaded for any future court case. The accident had occurred at 5 p.m., and it was now 1 a.m. This was happily the last DWI arrest of my 26-year career.

I turned on my emergency lights as I stopped behind a vehicle with their flashers on in the right lane. They were waiting on a wrecker, so for easier visibility and safety from oncoming vehicles, I stayed parked behind them. A car passed by and someone yelled out the window "C'mon officer! It's Christmas!" as he believed that I was on a traffic stop.

Things are not always as they seem.

I stopped a motorist for driving 20 over the limit. The driver told me that he had a Georgia DL, but not with him. It is important to watch a driver without ID sign his citation, as in this case the truth revealed itself when by force of habit, he signed his real name of "Ivan", then crossed it off and signed with the false full name that he had given me. I pointed out the error, to which he attempted to dismiss it by explaining that he was just nervous. I told him nervous or not, no amount of nervousness would cause you to sign a different name. Then more hooey spilled from his mouth when I heard "I'm going to

be honest with you. When I was younger, I used to sign my brother's name on tickets". I used some harsh language to get him to provide his true name. He had four warrants for IBC (Issuance of Bad Checks. Yes, people used to get arrested for "bounced" checks because banks did not provide overdraft protection as a customer courtesy), four other ticket warrants, a suspended driver license, and my added charge of Failure to ID as a Fugitive.

While waiting for the wrecker to hook up, I held up one of the arrestee's business cards that I found while searching his vehicle and said "So, REVEREND, do you make a habit out of lying to the police?"

"No Sir."

"Then why did you lie to me?"

"I didn't want to go to jail."

"What kind of moral example are you for the members of your flock?"

"I was weak sir. I'm human. I make mistakes." He asked me if I was a Christian, and I said that I was. He queried "Have you been saved?" This bothered me that a man like him who violated a profession that I had held in high esteem and had diminished his professional integrity was now trying to take the moral high ground. I just replied "Don't even start."

A couple was caught by loss prevention trying to steal $220 of merchandise from a department store. The female thief alone had over $500 cash in her purse, which I'm sure she wished she had used as she contemplated their situation while being transported to jail.

I was working my Sam's Club job when I noticed two girls about 8 years old at a cash register 20 yards in front of me. They were whispering, smiling, and giggling, and I could see that they were looking at me and that they wanted to say something to me. I waved and smiled at them. One girl started to meekly walk toward me, then chickened out and retreated back to her friend. Then, after they spoke to their mothers, they both walked over and in unison waved and said "Hello", then giggled and scurried back to the register lane. Moments later, they returned and blurted simultaneously "Thank you for saving the world!" I smiled and thanked them, but needed to correct that flattering absurdity.   I told them that they probably meant to thank me for serving the people of Dallas. One of them smiled

and said timidly and meekly "Yeah, that's what we meant," then

they ran back to join their mothers.

Most police officers have a soft spot for kids and the elderly.

A teenaged male kept hanging around listening to me speak

with potential witnesses to an apartment burglary that had just

occurred. The teenager gave me a description of someone that

he saw running from the scene. Turned out he was

hoodwinking me and just trying to throw me off his trail. An

actual witness to the burglary called 911 and they had me call

her. The woman alerted me that the teenager that I was talking

to was actually the burglar. I arrested him.

When I worked my Sam's Club job, I would occasionally take

a brief walk in the parking garage for a security check. Once I

was walking and noticed a woman walking slower up ahead of

me. A teenage boy was walking faster than me and as he overtook me on my left, I asked if he could do me a favor and see if he could help that woman find her car. The naivete of youth; I didn't think he would be so gullible as to actually rush up and ask the woman if he could help her find her car. It was supposed to be comical. He was supposed to just smile or guffaw at the suggestion of it. The woman told him in a perturbed tone "I didn't drive here!" The expression on the boy's face betrayed his bewilderment. Only then did a light bulb go off in the boy's head that the woman was wearing dark sunglasses and was blind or legally blind, and was using a long white collapsible walking stick to tap her way around. I was aghast that he actually did it and apologized to him, but he was too embarrassed and scurried away without saying anything.

I was taking a break from bicycling in hot weather and was enjoying a free fruit drink from a liquor store on the north end of White Rock Lake. A man walked in and when he was in line waiting to buy more alcohol, he engaged me in conversation wanting to talk about the Obama/McCain Presidential election, but his breath and his eyes disclosed his inebriation. Never talk to a Police Officer in a public place when you're drunk, and in this man's case, wanting to be more of a drunkard. He had driven drunk to the liquor store (though I had not seen that), but he would not drive home drunk. I arrested him and had another bike officer bring his police car so we could haul him for public intoxication.

Along the way he commented that he didn't like girls because they gave you diseases and stuff, that even a condom doesn't work sometimes and that you can still get AIDS. He would rather just stay at home with his penis pump, and play with himself in front of the TV than be out with a woman, it was a lot cheaper. It was a hard sell and we were unconvinced. The crazy outlandish things people can say when they've over imbibed with alcohol.

An accident had caused enough damage to a car that it had to be towed due to leakage. The pale 20-year-old male driver seemed disoriented and confused. I told him to take anything of value from his vehicle before we towed it, so he removed his long black leather jacket from the trunk and wore it over his waist-length black leather jacket, despite the 70-degree temperature. I searched his vehicle prior to towing and he had a black leather lace up corset in his backpack. The other officer said his DL picture looked like he was a woman. He was lost and confused about who he was and was having a gender identity crisis.

At near 2 p.m., a male parked his car alongside a gate entry key pad outside an apartment complex vehicle gate, then stepped out and entered the complex through a pedestrian gate. An off duty Dallas PD Reserve Officer who lived at the complex observed this and walked over to speak to the occupants and pointed out what should have been obvious, that they were in a bad spot and were preventing tenants in other vehicles from having key pad access so the gate would open. To his surprise, there was a chrome pistol in plain view atop the center console. He ordered the two occupants out at gunpoint, and called 911.

They were still sprawled out on the pavement when we arrived code 3, and we handcuffed and searched them. The Reserve Officer searched the vehicle which would be towed and he found another pistol, a .380 with 3 rounds in the magazine beneath the driver's seat. But we still had no driver. Minutes later a male appeared on the other side of the entrance gate and inquired "What's going on?" The Reserve Officer recognized him as having been the driver that exited the vehicle minutes earlier. I had an approaching tenant use the keypad to open the traffic gate for us, and the inquisitive driver was arrested for UCW (Unlawful Carry Weapon), as was the female from the middle of the backseat who insisted that the chrome pistol on the console belonged to her.

While working security at my Sam's Club job, I noticed (as did most everyone I suppose) that a customer in a check-out line resembled a band member of the rock group ZZ Topp, as he sported the trademark long squared off beard and dark sunglasses. He walked past me to get a soda from a vending machine and kindly asked if I wanted one. I thanked him but declined. As he passed me again, I said

"You must like their music?" "Whose?" "ZZ Topp." He smiled, and replied "Oh yeah...I'm one of 'em". I thought to myself "Sure you are buddy," then added "I guess you could tell anybody that because I don't know what they look like up close." He smiled again, then admitted "Yeah, I guess I could", then stepped back in line. The store manager walked over and told me that he really was a ZZ Topp band member who lived in Dallas and shopped there about once a month. After he checked out and was leaving the store with his groceries, I apologized to him and shook his hand. We introduced ourselves, and he was Dusty Hill, the guitar player. He graciously signed the back of one of my business cards. He shopped there two days later and talked to me some more after buying me a Mountain Dew. He was a talented, nice and good man.

I pulled a woman over for an expired registration. I thought that I must've ran the wrong license plate at first because it had expired 3 years and 9 months earlier, but I hadn't. The woman explained that it kind of became an experiment to see how long she could go without having to pay for a new registration sticker. I'd say her experiment was successful.

Someone called police about two well-dressed white males kicking in the door of an apartment. The call didn't sound right. People who are well-dressed are not typically burglars. Sure enough, they were two suburban detectives who came to the complex to execute a felony burglary warrant, but they violated police protocols and professional courtesy by not waiting for Dallas PD who they requested for assistance to have a uniformed presence. They kicked in the front door and the felon they sought simply crawled out a back window and got away, because no one was watching the back. They were lucky that they were not shot upon entry because they didn't wear any immediately recognizable uniformed police clothing.

How many more crimes would their escaped suspect commit before his capture because of their impatience and carelessness? The other uniformed officer and I shook our heads at each other in disbelief.

According to our call, a man was in a parking garage and refused to leave. I was surprised by that very simple comment because it did not indicate that our suspect was wearing a pink dress, purple shoes, a wide white frilly hat, a large white pearled necklace, nail and toenail polish, and wore lipstick. No Las Vegas male "showgirl" performer, he really made for an unattractive woman. I patted him down for officer safety and removed his two little breasts from his bra after I squeezed them; they were two rolls of socks.

He went to jail for warrants and was put into a jail jumpsuit before being placed in the male holdover area to avoid harassment from other arrestees.

I volunteered for a disturbance call, and seconds later the dispatcher added that the suspect was last seen running naked through the apartment complex. I arrived and began to drive around, then spotted a maintenance man waiting for me in a parking lot. He pointed out the man who was now standing by his car and thankfully was fully clothed. I was told that he was drunk, and after getting dressed had pulled down his pants briefly to urinate in public. He was obviously drunk when I made contact and could hardly stand, speaking slowly and slurring his words. I cuffed him and placed him in the squad car.

I recovered his wallet from his car and noticed a used case of Heineken beer on the back seat.

On the way to Detox, the arrestee asked "Sir, let me tell you something. Why are you arresting me?"

"Because you're publicly intoxicated."

"Why are you arresting me? What does that mean?"

"You are drunk outside."

"But why are you arresting me?" He became more annoying, asking me the same question so I ignored him. He just kept asking, so I turned up the music. After a couple of minutes, he stopped talking.

At Detox I had to laugh a bit because he wasn't following instructions. He was told to put both of his hands on the counter, but repeatedly lifted one hand off the counter to point at me and tried to say something. Each time that he did-- nearly ten times--the City Marshal's Office Jailer would grab his hand

and slap it back onto the counter telling him not to move his hands. He was speechless without the use of that hand.

   A woman had been working outside doing yard work, and left her overhead garage door open for convenience. She went back into her house. She walked through her living room, then noticed a shadow from her peripheral vision. She looked and saw a man standing in a corner trying to hide and be invisible. He was next to her now open jewelry box on a china cabinet. She ran back outside screaming "I'm being robbed! Help! I'm being robbed!" Her 17-year-old daughter heard her mother's pleas for help and pressed the panic alarm button inside the house. The suspect had run outside too, and trailed her by several yards. She shouted "Stop him!" to some tree cutters that she had just hired fifteen minutes earlier. One of the tree cutters was holding a chainsaw in one hand and tried unsuccessfully to push the fleeing suspect to the ground. The skinny suspect-- who appeared to be high on drugs-- ran to his

car a little further up the street. The tree cutter and a passerby
ran after him and memorized the license plate number as he
drove away. The suspect had stolen three rings and about ten
gold and silver necklaces.

This was the only residential panic alarm in my 26 years in
patrol that was not a false alarm.

I stopped a driver for not wearing his seatbelt. He was
actually test driving the vehicle with the owner sitting next to
him. The vehicle also had an expired inspection, expired
registration, and no insurance. I felt his first name probably
gave him enough grief in his life, so he didn't receive any tickets
that day.

Finally, his first name of "Spanky" brought him some good
luck.

Some punk kids had decided to dump urine and excrement into a library book return chute, and smeared the feces all over the inside of the book drop so that most all the books and video tapes returned by borrowers came into contact with the fecal matter. Because of the bio-hazard nature of the crime, the library supervisor believed that irreparable damage had been done and that most of the estimated $2000 worth of books and tapes could not be salvaged.

I pulled over a vehicle with a warrant hit on the license plate. It belonged to a female passenger who I arrested. The driver had a suspended driver license and was also arrested. We were going to release the car to a licensed driver, but neither of the two males in the back seat had a license, nor did the two people that arrived to drive it away ten minutes later. We towed it.

At about 9 p.m. one night, I drove into a parking lot at a lake because there were a dozen cars and I wondered what could be happening so late. I saw a group sitting among several picnic tables and walked into their midst. Eerily strange, I was the only one moving; all were seated motionless and no one was uttering a word. One guy was standing still in the parking lot. I could see one male walking downhill to join a group of about 25 walking silently near the lake. It had a creepy zombie-like feel to it.

I asked aloud "Is everything alright?" A girl at a picnic table looked up slowly and broke the hushed stillness and said "We're having a prayer walk." I had never heard of such a thing until then.

I spotted a truck parked in the grass along a stretch of road with signs that read "No Parking, Tow Away Anytime." I stood behind it with a ticket book in hand. I saw two fishing poles in the bed, did a visual scan, and saw a couple fishing about 50 yards away. I pointed at the truck, but had no reaction from them. No one waved, or put down their poles. I started to write the ticket, and only then did the man walk over to me and declare "I'll move it now officer." I told him he was too late, he had already ignored all of the signs and parked there anyway. Unsettled, he was angry that he was getting a ticket, and told me that I should be out at the lake catching rapists or something. I told him that we didn't have any, and hadn't for the 5 years that I'd worked here. He turned away and muttered "Fucking ass wipe!" I told him that I'd take his ID for that. Now in disbelief again, he gave it to me and asked why he was receiving another ticket, as I opened a different ticket book. "Profanity in the Park" was my reply. Now he was more upset, but I was happier. By the time I finished writing that ticket, he had time to think and had calmed down. As he signed, he kindly said "Officer, I really appreciate what you do."

I took a call one night at the lake that involved a driver window being down and the car horn blaring non-stop. I arrived to find a male slumped over the steering wheel with his head resting on the horn. I thought that he must be dead from a murder or a suicide, but I saw no blood. I saw something metallic in his hand, and took it out; it was the car cigarette lighter. I placed my hand on his shoulder and he awakened with a startle. I asked if he was okay, and he said that he was just tired. I took his ID, and had him step outside of his car so that I could get a better visual of the inside. No alcohol or drugs in plain sight, no marijuana odor, and he was not a diabetic. Now alert, he was sent home to sleep in his bed instead of in his car in the park at 9:45 p.m.

We responded to a call one night from concerned parents whose 3-year-old daughter on several occasions had told them that a strange man had stood in her room at night, having climbed down from the attic and emerged from her closet. The parents had checked a couple of times to pacify her, but dismissed her fear as the product of an active imagination. However, their little girl continued to insist that a man was entering her room, so they wanted us to search the attic. I

pushed the overhead door away to the attic, then stepped onto

some closet shelves to peer into and shine my flashlight in all

directions. No sign of disturbed or compressed insulation, no

footprints. I assured the parents that no one had been up

there.

They thanked me for easing their minds, and admitted that

just before their call they had been drinking beer and watching

horror movies all night.

I arrived at a major accident call, and asked one of the drivers

for her name. She gave me a name, then added that she had

both a TX DL and ID card but that they were at home. After

getting her date of birth I searched for her DL on the computer

but none was found. Returning, I again requested her name

and she gave me the same one as before. I asked if she had

something in her purse with her name on it, and she replied no

but I was welcome to look in it if I wanted. I didn't hesitate and found a health card with a different name and birthday on it.

When queried, she admitted to the truth. Under her actual

name she had a Probation Violation warrant. Her lie to me also

gave her a charge of Failure to ID as a Fugitive.

On New Year's Eve 1997, I was working a small party at a

White Rock Lake park rental building that only involved about

25 Lutheran Church Members. The organizer brought me a

plate of food as I watched over their cars in the parking lot, and

told me that because I was giving up my New Year's Eve to be

with them, that he would pay me an extra $5/hr. A few minutes

to midnight, I walked inside the building for the countdown.

A few minutes afterwards I went back outside to the legal fire

that I had started in a designated fire pit. I wore a pullover cap

and gloves on this quiet, cold, starlit night. I enjoyed the

warmth from the fire. I listened to the periodic crackle of

celebratory fireworks and gunshots echoing from the distance

around the lake for the next 20 minutes. Ah, memories.

It was a rare February day, having snowed all day yesterday and half the night, and only reached a high in the upper 30's. We were taking truants to school and my partner hit the brakes hard to allow a woman with soiled pants to cross the street. We checked on her and she was a MHMR (Mental Health Mental Retardation) person. We found out that she lived at an apartment complex across the street, and had other officers take her there. They told her to stay inside her apartment. When we returned and drove down the same street, we saw the same woman standing on a corner near a school. No bus stop, no ride, just standing in the cold wearing one glove. I spoke to her emergency contact from her lease info, and she was a schizophrenic in denial who didn't like to take her meds. We brought her to the Psych Unit at Parkland Hospital and nearly gagged from the overwhelming odor that she was emitting; she was menstruating, and the stench was a mixture of her blood and fecal matter. One of the orderlies there commented that she definitely needed to be there for help.

I was taking a break inside a liquor store, drinking a free non-alcoholic drink. My squad car was parked at the front door parking space. A man walked inside, and the clerk motioned to me with his hand about this male, and I knew from his having done this before that he believed the male to be drunk. The man brought a beer to the counter and the clerk refused to sell to him because he had been drinking. "Oh, c'mon man, just sell me the beer so I can get outta here." The clerk refused again. I intervened, and arrested him for public intoxication. He cooperated, thinking that was his only charge, but he had two felony warrants too. He had walked past a squad car to enter the liquor store drunk while having felony warrants, proof that alcohol kills brain cells.

As I was about to leave a parking lot, I did a registration check of a vehicle entering the parking lot that passed me. Someone in that car had received tickets in the past that were now outstanding warrants. I U-turned and flipped on my emergency lights when I stopped behind the vehicle that was now in a Billiards hall parking lot spot. The driver had just stepped inside the front door of the business, in spite of my believing that he had seen me. He had just sat down on a bar stool when I confronted him for ID, which he said he didn't have. When asked his name, he responded with the name of the male listed on all of the outstanding warrants. I had him step back outside with me. I told him that normally on traffic stops when we confirm warrants for an arrest, we would tow the car, but in this case since he was already in a parking space I would leave it here with his friend, providing I had his permission and his cooperation. I went back to my car and was on the phone confirming some of his ticket warrants when I saw him hurriedly slip back inside the billiards hall front door. I then saw through the glass that he gave his car keys to his friend, but was alarmed when I lost sight of him from the tinted glass and window promotions that obstructed my view. I waited a few seconds more to see if he came back outside, but then hung up the phone to check on his whereabouts. I asked his friend where he went, and he lied when he told me that he thought he was in the bathroom. Some other customers were honest and helpful and told me that someone ran out the back door. I informed the friend of his fleeing friend's stupid judgement and the consequences, took the keys back, and he told me the full name to confirm his friend's identity. I also found his name and address on his auto insurance card. Now I towed his car, typed up an extra charge of Evading Detention for the next time he was stopped, and he still had his outstanding warrants.

Some people deal with their problems, some compound them by pouring gasoline on the fire.

It was raining, and a driver made an error and caused a three-car accident. A couple of off duty officers didn't witness the accident, but they heard the crash and saw cars spinning and debris flying. After the cars had come to a stop, one driver flung his door open and with a burst of speed, ran down an alley behind a row of houses. The officers drove down the street and paralleled the suspect as they could see him running in the same direction down the alley. When the officers got to the end of the street, they exited their car and waited for the suspect to emerge from the alley. When he did, they loudly identified themselves by brusquely saying "Police!" as they focused their pistols on him and ordered him to the ground.

This accident was our call, and we had been told by some witnesses that some people from the accident were pointing pistols at someone else involved in the accident. We arrived and fortunately recognized that the two-armed civilians were actually two known officers. We handcuffed the suspect and took him back to the accident scene. Two people from the other cars had been taken to a hospital for injuries. We discovered that the only reason that our suspect had ran was because he had no car insurance and he had caused the accident. What would have been a simple no insurance citation at that time had he remained at the scene became two felony charges of FSRA (Failed to Stop and Render Aid) when he failed to assist the accident victims that went to the hospital.

A well-dressed man had just returned to his apartment, having over $400.00 that he had just cashed from his first paycheck. Seconds, later, there was a knock on the door. He asked "Who is it?" but never waited for a response and opened it. Immediately, he was stepping backwards into his apartment when a .38 pistol was pointed at his head. Two suspects burst into his apartment as he stumbled backwards to his bedroom and fell onto his bed.

"Give us your money mother fucker! Give us your money!" demanded the suspects. The man reached into his inner suit coat pocket to withdraw his cash in a bank envelope. One of suspects panicked and shouted "He's going for a gun!" and the man believed that at that moment he was going to die. The man handed over his cash to one of the suspects. He was then struck once on the left eye, and twice on the right side of his head, probably first with a fist, then followed up by the butt end of a pistol. The complainant now had a pillow shoved down on top of his face and heard one of the suspects say excitably "Let's Shoot him!" The other suspect was the voice of reason and responded "No, we got what we want." The suspects began to leave, and the victim heard one say "I still got the gun on you mother fucker! You better not even move!" One of the suspects took a picture off of a dining room wall but decided not to take it (that was later dusted for latent prints). The man arose from his bed after about ten seconds and observed the two suspects get into a vehicle with two other males in the back seat, then drove away.

A woman went out looking for her ex-boyfriend. He broke up with her two weeks earlier to get back together with the mother of his child. She found his car in a parking lot near where he lived. He overheard some talking in the parking lot and looked out his window to see her pouring a can of Pepsi onto his car's finish. He rushed outside "Bitch! What's wrong with you?" She already flattened two of his tires. She moved toward him to strike him, and he held both of her arms to prevent getting hit. Powerless while restrained, the woman leaned forward and bit him on his left check, leaving a lower jaw teeth mark that was an open bleeding wound. She left when he went back to his apartment to call the police, but told him that she wasn't finished with him yet.

The victim said that he was on probation and didn't want any trouble.

I took a call regarding several 10-12 year-old girls taking turns driving a golf cart up and down the streets. I arrived to the area and found the golf cart parked on the grass several yards away from the streets. The girls and a woman were standing next to it. I informed the woman--who was the mother of the 12-year-

old-- that the golf cart wasn't street legal and those driving it

could receive citations. The 12-year-old asked if she could drive

the cart back across the street to a visible garage. This was just

a two-lane road, but I told her that I would prefer that a

licensed driver do it because there were still cars passing by

every ten seconds or so. The mother was a licensed driver,

though her husband was the golf cart owner and she didn't

know how to drive it. Her daughter gave her some simple

instructions, but neglected to mention one important tidbit.

Like a cartoon, the mother sat in the cart ready to go forward

but when she stepped on the gas pedal, the cart was in reverse

and she surged backwards until she hit a small tree. This

caused her a pronounced head whiplash. Fighting back tears,

she drove the golf cart home after putting it in forward gear.

I stopped an SUV because a registration check showed to

have been expired for 15 months. When I walked up to the

driver side, I leaned forward to notice the expired registration sticker and also an inspection sticker that had been expired for eight months. As I did so, the driver said aloud "Jackpot!" He said that he knew about the expirations, and he had just taken his chances. He smiled, and told me to do my duty, and that if anybody deserved a ticket, he did. He mentioned that once while driving thru a quiet tranquil suburb he was stopped by the police three times in one week, but this was his first time in Dallas. Still smiling and with a great attitude, he signed both of his tickets and was back on his way.

I had just dismounted from my bicycle at the front of a 7-11 and took off my helmet. I inhaled and smelled the odor of burning marijuana. A female had just opened her driver door and closed it, then stepped into the store. A male remained seated on the front passenger seat. I went to the car and pulled open the door on his side, and again smelled the marijuana. The male at first denied having smoked marijuana but then admitted that he had done so earlier. He was insistent that he had been the only one, and that the driver hadn't smoked any. I asked for his ID, and he handed me his TDC Card (Texas Department of Corrections ID, always a red flag that raised the alert of any Texas Officer). My bicycle officer partner was behind me providing cover, and I told him what I had. I had the male stand at the front of the vehicle and gave him a quick pat down for officer safety, and the female who had just stepped out of the 7-11 joined him. I searched the car for marijuana while my partner watched them, but none was found. I did, however, find a pistol under the male's seat. It looked real enough, but was a Daisy BB pistol, not the 9MM automatic that it appeared to be at first glance. The ex-con denied having any knowledge that it was there, attributing it to "kids" that had been playing in the car that day and the day earlier. I didn't believe him and thought that he might be robbing people with his realistic-looking BB pistol. I did a Suspicious Person report and notified a detective in the Robbery Section.

A reckless father was enjoying himself at the lake with his wife and infant son, evidenced by the big smile on Dad's face. He was foolishly putting his son's life at risk, riding his bicycle down the concrete bicycle trail with one hand on his handlebar, while the other was on his son's foot...with his son riding on his shoulders! I stopped him and lectured him for his stupidity, then wrote him a no bicycle helmet citation.

I later spoke to a jail sergeant who told me that under those circumstances he would have approved an arrest report for a felony charge of Endangering a Child.

A manager at Sam's Club told me that a strange young man was inside the employee break room. No one knew him, and he was acting weird. I began walking that way, but was told that he was out in the store again. I spied him walking my way wearing I-phone earplugs. I tried talking to him, but he was jumping around to the beat of his music, and either couldn't hear me, or ignored me. I removed one of his earplugs, and told

him that he needed to have a membership card to shop there,

and some customers had complained that he was acting

strange. "Man, I'm just listening to my I-phone." The manager

informed him that he needed to leave. The male put the

earplug back into his ear, and I thought that he was going to

follow us to the front door. Instead, I looked back after a few

steps and he had turned right and was now looking at some

packages of meat. This time I physically escorted him to the exit

door by grabbing an arm. I removed his lime green employee

cart boy mesh vest that he had taken and was wearing. I also

removed a blue 2011 Mavericks Championship shirt that he was

wearing from the store (I hadn't given him a chance to pay for

it, not that he would have). I looked at his name on his ID in his

wallet for my report, but had to rush forward to put it back in

his pant pocket when he started to walk away without it.

A few minutes later inside the store, a young man asked me

if I may have seen his friend. After I asked for a description, I explained that I had escorted him out, and told him why. "He did all that?" He said his friend had some mental problems, and I assumed that he and his buddy were supposed to be watching him. I pointed them in the right direction and they returned to the store twice in two hours to ask if I had seen him. I told them to contact the man's parents to see if they wanted the police to make a report. I could tell they were reluctant to do that, having been remiss of their duty for not having kept their eyes on him. Out they went to search for him again.

A 17-year-old male robbed a bank at gunpoint. Just as he left the bank a dye-pack exploded in his money bag, and he was inked and frightened. He ran a few blocks and stepped into a small bar on a bright sunny summer day. I was first to enter the bar, and went to the larger part of the room in a pistol scan position. We were temporarily blinded by several seconds of darkness before our eyes could adjust to the dimly lit establishment. Another officer found him hiding in the bathroom and I rushed to assist with his arrest.

We were thankful that we were not shot during our entry because of our initial loss of vision.

A 14-year-old boy was living with his grandparents in a nice neighborhood because his mother was in prison for drug possession. Any anger or resentment he felt should certainly not have been directed at his loving grandparents. His grandparents told him that there was no school that day, but the boy responded by saying that he had band practice. His grandmother wouldn't let him leave the house with his expensive musical instrument, fearing he would sell it to get money for drugs, as a few other things had already been missing from their house. The boy was not deterred, and still insistent with his oft repeated lie "I got to practice! I got to practice!" Grandma was wise to his excursion, and asked him to leave the instrument in the house, and to go back inside. The boy had a short temper and was impatient with this parenting, so he yelled "Get out of my way bitch! Get your mother-fucking ass out of my way!" Grandma confiscated the musical instrument from her grandson, but he shoved her away into a wall, and left the house upset and empty-handed.   We couldn't locate him and filed the Family Violence Assault on him at large.

I arrived at the front of a middle school where about 30 students were protesting, some with handmade placards. I asked them why they were not in class and I was told that the Assistant Principal was rude and treated minority students unfairly when it came to school suspensions and punishment. There was one adult with them, the self-appointed protest leader. I informed the students that they had a right to protest, but not during school hours. By state law, they were required to be in school during school hours; if they wanted to protest, they needed to do it before or after class on their own time. They needed to all go back to class or they would be issued tickets for "Disruption of School Activities." I had got their attention, but having safety in numbers, they ignored me and continued to protest. I requested backup to assist me in writing citations, and about ten police cars showed up, including some Dallas Public Schools officers. Some indecisive Sergeants who appeared were reluctant to make a decision and erred on the side of caution by contacting a Lieutenant. It was finally decided--surprise--that the kids needed to go back to their classrooms or they would get a ticket. Faced with that ultimatum, they returned to class and no citations were issued. The students had done more than an hour of protesting and felt like their voices had been heard.

On October 3, 1995, the much-awaited verdict of "Innocent" was read out at the double murder trial of ex-Pro Football Superstar O.J. Simpson. At that time, I was at the county jail processing an arrestee, and most of us were crowded around a TV at the time the verdict was read. I noticed that whether

police officers cheered or were disappointed and upset,
depended on whether the officer was black or white
respectively.

    I had just brought an arrestee to our city jail for unpaid tickets and was returning to my patrol division area. Just a couple of blocks away, I did a license plate check and a warrant hit appeared for a female, and there was a female driver. I did a traffic stop and the warrants were for her. She started to cry and said that she just got a job and she would lose it if she got arrested. She had been trying to take care of the tickets but she didn't have the money, she hadn't worked in several months, and she didn't know how she would buy Christmas presents for her two little girls. I wrote her a ticket for No Insurance, and then found out on the computer that her DL had been suspended for over a year for—No Insurance. I had another officer cover me and we took her to jail for a suspended DL, her ticket warrants, and I had her car towed.

Her situation bothered me enough that I submitted her name to our Santa Cops program, so that she would receive several Christmas presents for her girls and some bags of food near Christmas.

I had a call about a car that had crashed into an apartment one early evening. I was guessing that maybe a few bricks were chipped off a corner, or a dent in the wall. I arrived instead to find that a car was completely inside a living room! A male in his 60's that lived next door had decided that rather than bring his cleaning supplies to his car, he was going to bring his car to his apartment. He drove over the parking lot curb, onto the grass and sidewalks, and coasted to stop near his apartment door. The problem was that he then stepped on the accelerator and not the brake (two-footed driving?). He quickly surged forward and crashed through the wall of his next-door neighbor, where a woman had been watching TV on the couch. Incredibly, no one was injured, but she and others in the apartment were naturally shaken and frightened. At one point I had to step outside to quell an argument that had started between the male residents from the destroyed apartment and the reckless driver. One of the women from the apartment took my advice and had gone across the street to buy a disposable camera to take pictures of the car and damaged property. I gave the driver's auto insurance card to the family. They were concerned about what would happen if I couldn't contact the complex manager or the maintenance man because it was a Sunday and they couldn't live like that. I told them in that case, they would have to go to Home Depot and buy some plywood to nail over the hole in the wall and stay with some friends or relatives until the morning when the office would reopen. These were section 8 tenants and they were surprised that they might have to help themselves and not have everything provided for them. Did they want a paid hotel stay? Fortunately, I made contact with the apartment complex manager and a maintenance man made a temporary plywood wall after the car was successfully extricated.

A young thug was driving too fast and lost control of the stolen vehicle, rolling over a residential street curb, then over a fire hydrant, then a street sign, and finally stopped abruptly when he struck a tree. Not wearing a seat belt, he was thrown forward over the steering wheel and his head slammed into the front window, causing a bloodied glass bubble. He was injured, but not unconscious, and after some seconds elapsed he got out of the car and began to run. A young neighbor had witnessed this and chased the suspect, catching up to and tackling him in a back yard. The suspect squirmed and struggled to get away, and managed to escape his grasp. However, in the process, he lost his long sleeve shirt and pants, and was now running thru the neighborhood in red and green boxer shorts. It was a weekend morning and not many people were active yet. He was seen again a few blocks away when he tried to steal two cars, and was seen entering someone's open garage.

Despite the manhunt involving three police cars and the police chopper, he eluded capture, more than likely from stealing another car. We never even laid eyes on him.

A car chase ended not with a wreck, but when the car thief realized that he couldn't outdrive or shake the police, so he simply and smartly pulled over and stopped to surrender. He was 13.

I ran the registration of a Mercedes that I saw parked in a park, and thought that I must've misread the license plate. I circled back around and stepped out to look at the VIN. It matched the plates lying face up on the back seat. There was no owner present, but 1½ hours later I spotted a woman driving this vehicle and did a traffic stop. I explained what the problem was and I did her a favor and removed the displayed license plate, and attached the correct plates from her backseat. She told me that she had recently bought the vehicle with what were the wrong license plates. The dealership must have

depleted their supply of temporary paper tags and decided to

just put any license plates on the vehicle, knowing they would

soon have the new plates ready for her. The plates that the

dealership had fastened to her car belonged to a 34-year-old

Chevy with a registration sticker that had expired 22 years

earlier.

I wrote a ticket to a male driver for running a red light. Hours

later I walked out 50 yards into the park and asked the owner of

a vehicle why he got to park on the grass when everyone else

had to park in a parking lot. He moved his car. An hour later I

observed a vehicle turn right at a stop sign without stopping

first. I U-turned and pulled him over. It was the same man who

had parked up on the grass earlier. This time I wrote him a

citation. I returned to my vehicle and noticed the extreme

coincidence from the only two citations I wrote that day; both

of the driver first names were "Demetrius".

I did a welfare check on a male from a call one October day. It involved a decades-long homeless alcoholic by the nick name of "Bar-B-Q- Bob". I don't know how he received that nickname, or even "Bob", because his name was neither Bob nor Robert. He was intoxicated and had urinated on himself. He wanted an ambulance to take him to a hospital so that he could get treated for his alcoholism, but admitted that if he ever got into a Detox program, he would go back to drinking after he was released. He said that his liver was shot, and that he needed a new one. I reminded him that as long as he stayed an alcoholic, that no one would ever give him a new liver. Collectively and conservatively, he had been arrested by Dallas Officers hundreds of times for Public Intoxication over decades, no exaggeration. I put him in the backseat of my cruiser and took him to Detox once more. Upon arrival, I had him step out, and I tried to yank up his pants because he told me they were falling down. I couldn't get a good grip as they were wet and heavier from his absorbed urine (He had peed himself in my car during the trip, which I cleaned up later with some cleaning room supplies). I expected him to hang onto his waistband by using his hands which were behind his back. He didn't. We took a few more steps and his pants dropped to his ankles in daylight. I held onto his arm as he shuffled the 20 more yards to the door. A City Marshals Office (also known as "Detox") employee stepped out as we entered and exclaimed "How can he be here so soon? We just released him this morning". It was 5:30 p.m.

He was cantankerous and ornery, but usually not a danger to anyone. He lived a truly pathetic existence.

My rookie and I stopped a vehicle at night. It was a young mother and her 5-year-old son, who was seated in a child seat in the right rear seat. He saw me standing outside the car on his side. Eyes wide, he lowered his window and asked concernedly "Are you going to arrest us?"

We received a call about a suspicious male walking in a

neighborhood. The other officer spotted the tattoo-covered,

skinny-legged, muscular-topped male coming out of an alley.

We checked him for warrants, but he was clear. He was

nervous, and out-of-place in this nice neighborhood, but we had

no reason to detain to him and cut him loose. Hours later, I

took an attempted stolen vehicle report from an old man who

lived just one block from where we had earlier detained the

suspicious male in the alley. It turned out the old guy rented

out a room to our suspicious male's sister and mother. Our 25-

year-old suspect from earlier had just been released from

prison, and his palm print was found inside of the vehicle that

he had tried to steal. I searched the neighborhood but couldn't

find him.

Weeks later, I was watching the news and I saw our suspect

picture on TV. He had been stopped by police while driving a

stolen car and was arrested for that and Fraudulent Use or

Possession of Identifying Information. He had nearly 30

checkbooks, credit cards, credit card applications, and ID cards,

all with the names of other people both real and imagined.

An officer from a southern Texas town that bordered the Gulf

of Mexico needed an officer to check on an address to hopefully

find and notify next-of-kin. He wanted them to call him so that

he could report the death of a man that resided at that home

address. I rang the doorbell and knocked but there was no

answer. I put a note inside the front door for someone to read

when a mailman approached. He informed me that the older

man who lived there had suspended his mail about 10 days

earlier, and that he thought that he lived alone. I now realized

that the tragic death was his own. I tried to get a valid phone

number from his burglar alarm permit, his water bill, and

neighbors, but to no avail. I left notes in the neighbors'

mailboxes because they weren't home. I learned of the older

man's fate when I called and spoke to a southern Texas

sergeant. The man had driven himself to the coast, intending to

kill himself by kayaking out into the ocean, but decided that

might be a frightening or agonizing death from exposure,

sharks, drowning, or dehydration, per his suicide note. Instead,

he shot himself in the head while facing the ocean.

A 15-year-old-girl ran away with her former Church Youth

Minister, aged 24 (he'd been fired), and was reported as a

runaway by her parents. The Border Patrol stopped the couple

when they were returning from Mexico, and the girl's parents

drove hundreds of miles to retrieve their daughter. Things were

fine for several days, and the girl was back in school again. But

the girl left a farewell note for her parents saying she was angry

at them for not allowing her to be with her boyfriend. Barefoot,

she left her bedroom where her dad had nailed the window

shut, then slipped out of the kitchen window, leaving footprints

in the mud below. She may have been carrying or wearing extra

clothes but her closet looked full. She did take all of her jewelry, but how valuable could the jewelry collection of a 15 year old have been?

My partner and I went to an address to look for a runaway believed by a detective to possibly be at the location. Problem was that each address in the complex had four apartments, and we didn't know if it was Apt. A, B, C, or D. In the correct breezeway, I noticed a male above us standing outside Apt. D. I ascertained that he was not our runaway. Interestingly, however, the apartment door was open and the dispersed odor of burning marijuana raised our awareness. We entered the apartment and found a 19-year-old sitting in his bedroom smoking weed with a baggie of marijuana at his feet. Marijuana is a depressant drug, but he sure became alert when he saw us. We never did finish looking for our runaway, but a drug user would do. Off to jail we went. At least we narrowed down the possibilities for the detective.

A friend hired me and several officers of my choosing to work

for him at an indoor concert that he had arranged featuring a

Persian Singer. All of the attendees were well-dressed.

Unfortunately, the concert was open to anyone who bought a

ticket, including a former employer of my friend with whom he

parted on negative terms. He made an appearance, and they

soon confronted each other and exchanged harsh words. Never

a good idea if you're the host, and an especially bad idea for the

other guy, knowing that the host was an ex-professional

kickboxer. My friend told him to leave, but he refused since he

had a ticket. Rather than refund his ticket, or have the police

that he hired to intervene, he resorted to an impulsive physical

response and roundhouse kicked the man to the ground. When

the man rose to his feet, my friend drop kicked him on the chest

and he fell back again. More loud heated words were

exchanged, and the man left with the encouragement of his

associate. I had not seen or heard of this fracas amid the din of

the concert. Another officer located me when someone had

told him. I heard the story from my friend, and I told him that he was lucky that his former employer had left the building. I told him that if his enemy was still present and wanted to make a police report, that I would've been forced to arrest him (my friend) for the assault. Surprised, he replied "But I hired you". I told him that he was the aggressor, and the other guy probably left because the carpet cushioned his fall and because he had been drinking and didn't want police intervention which could end with his arrest for drunkenness.

I spotlighted a vehicle in a park and a male had a cup that he put into the bed of his pickup truck. I stopped and saw that his girlfriend was drinking wine, and he was drinking from a quart of beer bottle. He put her cup down when he saw me. His ID check showed that he was a known offender for resisting arrest, so the dispatcher sent me some cover, and they arrived quickly. I confirmed the two felony warrants associated with his having resisted arrest, a Bond Forfeiture and an Insufficient Bond warrant. I arrested him and asked if he had anything on him that I should know about. His response was "Well, kind of". He

had a small single shot derringer in his right wind breaker

pocket. I wasn't sure how to unload it, so I handed it to one of

my officer friends who knew more about firearms than most

anyone I knew. Not many people have experience with

derringers, and like me, he couldn't open it to visually check the

chamber.

We arrived at the jail and found another officer to unload the

bullet before we went upstairs with our prisoner.

____

We responded to assist a Code Enforcement Officer who had

some difficulty with a pet owner at a home. While still outside,

we immediately detected the sharp putrid stench of urine as we

walked toward the house. The pet owner had one bedroom

window open in a failed attempt to aerate the room. She had

kept two large pythons there inside large plastic storage

containers. However, their un-caged food supply of over 30 rats

freely roamed the room, rat droppings and rat urine

everywhere on the carpet, with the window sill and curtains shredded from their gnawing.

The pet owner had a more conciliatory and cooperative attitude with the Code Enforcement Officer after we arrived.

A drunk male stumbled into a building and locked himself in the ladies restroom. I received permission and was about to kick the door open when a woman came with a key and unlocked it. The man was seated clothed on the toilet. I arrested him and took him to Detox. I'm pretty sure that he wasn't welcomed to attend the Alcoholics Anonymous meetings there anymore.

A personal home healthcare aide had been caring for an 87-year-old woman for two years. She started to have trouble breathing, and the labored breathing continued for 3 hours and didn't stop like it always did before. The next-door neighbor who had power of attorney was contacted, and she summoned

an ambulance. The frail woman stopped breathing before they

arrived. She was all bones and emaciated, weighing only 80

pounds. The last two years of her life was lived in her recliner

chair. She only got up to bathe and use the bathroom.

Otherwise, she slept there, watched TV and read there, ate

there....and died there. Her only living relative was an adopted

daughter that lived across the country, but an argument or

disagreement had prevented them from speaking to each other

for 25 years.

A man yelled to me from across the street. I drove over as he

was taking small backward steps while inside the open car door

of a woman as she slowly backed up trying to leave a parking

lot. I advised him not to risk serious injury to recover

merchandise like the $29 bottle of tequila this woman had

shoplifted from his store and had in her purse. She received a

theft ticket and he got his Tequila back.

I worked 4 hours at a Japanese Anime (animation) convention in downtown Dallas. A few people in costume told me and another officer that there was a man outside lying on the sidewalk, and he might have been beaten because there was blood too. We found a 35ish male, with some nasty dark purple vomit on the sidewalk. He said that he had a taco that hadn't agreed with him, but that he felt better. I remembered thinking that given the costume event inside, that maybe this skinny, pale, Gothic, vampire-like young man had tried to drink some blood. We called an ambulance for him, and then went upstairs to the office to get paid for our shift. I recited the story to those in the office, and said that a paramedic had said "He looks like a G.I." One of the women said "Gastro-intestinal." Seeing a chance for a joke, I said that I know that now but at the time I heard the paramedic say "He looks like a G.I.", that I had replied "He doesn't look like he's in the military to me." That brought laughter to the room.

A 20-year-old from Abilene was driving through Dallas when he got a flat tire. He had no spare. He checked his pockets and wallet, but he had no cash, no credit cards, no checks, just a nickel in one pocket. Rather than do something practical and legal, like soliciting someone for help, or going to Western Union to have money wired from his father, he decided on an imbecilic criminal option. He spied a 50ish woman walking down the sidewalk with a grocery bag in her hand, and walked from behind to catch up. While beside her, he struck up a conversation. The woman-- who lived in Iran most of the year-- later told me that she didn't fear him because he reminded her of her son. After lowering her guard and putting her at ease, he suddenly grabbed the shoulder strap of her purse and it quickly slid over her arm and he ran down the sidewalk with her stolen purse. The victim screamed, and two nearby maintenance men looked up and unflinchingly pursued the purse snatcher. Two blocks further, the suspect stopped running. Exhausted and fatigued, he told his captors "I give up! I give up! I can't run anymore!" They held him until a complex security officer arrived and handcuffed the thief. I arrived and returned the victim's purse along with the meager $16 cash that she had inside of it. She was grateful but also shocked and just wanted to go home to her daughter's apartment.

The 20-year-old prisoner was taken to jail. He had no criminal record, but didn't seem too concerned about his plight.

I later learned that the victim was so traumatized by the ordeal that she didn't want to be here in Dallas for the Theft from a Person trial.

____

Often, police officers may shift their focus during a suspect pat down from watching his hands and the area of his body that is being patted down to just the latter. I was literally directly across the street from the lobby of my Patrol Division when I did just that. As I was patting down my suspect and looking at his clothing as I did, the suspect said "Officer, are you looking for this?" I looked up and saw him holding a steak knife in his hand! "Give me that!" I exclaimed. The blade was not an illegal length but obviously could have ensured me serious bodily injury if he was violent. I was lucky that he didn't want to hurt me, and took the young man home to his parents as I had no criminal offense to arrest him.

While patrolling, I noticed a few people in the distance walking briskly between stores. At first, I thought that employees were exercising over their lunch break, but then I saw that a man in a black leather jacket was hustling far ahead of them and thought this may be a shoplifter. I informed the dispatcher of my location behind an electronics store, but he had no calls holding from that vicinity. I drove up and the vest-wearing employees told me that the thief up ahead had stolen something from the Sam's Club. I drove past the suspect and stepped out to confront him. He denied having stolen anything, and dismissed their accusations by saying that they just think he did. I got his ID and patted him down, finding a $230 portable

DVD player that was tucked into the front of his pants under his

tucked in t-shirt. The dispatcher now informed me that a

shoplift call had just come in from the Sam's Club. I could

proudly inform her that I had the suspect in custody.   Who says

there is never a cop when you need one?

At more than 50 years old, the arrestee was getting a bit old

to still be a crook. He had two prior theft convictions which

made this theft arrest a felony.

Driving through a parking lot at White Rock Lake, I saw a

doctor--still in his scrubs-- walking his dog unleashed in a grassy

strip by picnic tables and the shoreline. I stopped to remind him

to put his dog on leash and that was when his dog squatted to

defecate. I remained and the Doctor said "We'll take care of it."

I stayed. Again, he said that he would take care of it. I told him

that I would wait to make sure it was done, as I really didn't

think the good Doctor would clean up his dog's hot mess and

thought his facial expression confirmed it. He walked to his car

and returned with a napkin in each hand. I noticed that he had

walked several yards past where his dog had dropped

excrement and I suspected that he was looking for an old, dried

up pile that didn't stink and was easy to pick up. I stepped out

of my car and walked closer to help him out, then pointed and

said "It's right there." His wife helped him find it. He picked it

up and put it in the trash, then squatted and wiped his hands on

the grass. I said "Thank You". The wife asked me for my name,

which I gave. She realized that I could've written an unleashed

dog citation and said "Thank you officer, we're sorry." I thought

the experience was a humbling one for the Doctor; a wealthy

man who was reduced to cleaning up dog excrement that day.

I was walking out of a restaurant when a man told me about

an older male who had fallen in the parking lot. I could see that

a small, frail-looking old man was being helped to his feet and

into the truck of a good Samaritan who was going to take him home. Finding out where he lived, I told the good citizen that I would take him home and save him the trouble, since I had to go that way to get back to my beat. I checked with the dispatcher to see if she had any calls regarding this male, and she did, so she put that call "in my box". It seemed the 72-year-old man had visited a relative in South Dallas, but had got on the wrong bus and got off on the wrong street. He had been lost and was trying to make his way home when he fell. The man was an alcoholic, dirty, and had a stale beer smell. I supposed that he was drunk, but reasoned that if a citizen was going to take him home that it didn't seem right that I intervened and would take him to Detox instead.

His apartment door was closed but unlocked. I was shocked when I entered; where there should have been a dining room table, I counted twenty-five 12 &24 packs of beer and all of the empty beer cans in a large pile on the floor. All of those empty beer cans were like a metaphor of what had to have been an empty life. He had a dirty, stained couch from where he watched a small TV. In front of his couch was a coffee table with more empty beer cans and many used Kleenex--some with blood on them—several inches deep atop and around the bottom. His refrigerator was devoid of food, having only ketchup and mayonnaise packets.

I left then returned and brought him a couple of 7-11 sandwiches, and told management about how bleak his life was and that they should contact his emergency contact on file. I did a Social Services Referral and hoped he would receive some help.

He told me that he had decided to stop driving 6 years ago when he determined that he had to choose between driving and beer. He chose beer.

I was just leaving a house from a call when I noticed a car go past with expired tag and inspection stickers. I pulled out to catch up to her, but she was able to turn left before I could get behind her, and I had to yield to one car before I could turn left to follow. I hustled down the street and when I was almost at her car which she had parked along the street curb, she exited and started to walk behind her car. She pretended not to see me approaching as I stopped behind her car, now with my emergency lights on. As I exited my vehicle, she was walking across her front lawn. I called out "Ma'am, I need to see your driver's license and proof of financial responsibility." She played deaf and didn't respond and just kept walking toward her front door. I rushed up and now as I was behind her, I said the same thing. Again, I was ignored. Now alongside her, I asked if her DL and insurance were in the house, and she replied "No."

"Then where are you going?"

"Inside."

"No, you're not. This is an official traffic stop. You're not free to leave until I say you can leave."

"I know my rights'! You can't stop me. I got out of my car before you turned your lights on! I know the law!"

"You can't walk away because you feel like it or pretend like you couldn't hear me. You're being lawfully detained!"

She was still trying to open her front door, so I grabbed her by the arm and told her that she was going to wait for me back by her car, and I escorted her back. She stood there, visibly upset. I started to write her two tickets, and as I did so, her husband stepped outside and walked toward me. He didn't look hostile, but I stepped out of my car to meet him nevertheless. I explained to him what had transpired, and wondered aloud why she thought that she could just ignore me and walk into her house. He was cordial and told me that she sometimes had an attitude problem. Of course, he was not within earshot of his wife when he told me that.

In the early 1990's, I was assigned to White Rock Lake to work with a few Dallas Police Park Rangers. One of them and me were the first bicycle officers at the North East Patrol Division. During the year or so that I was there, we would occasionally assist our Vice section with Public Lewdness arrests by working undercover in the woods and public restrooms. Too many adult men would sometimes frequent these woods and restrooms and linger much longer than it took to find wildflowers (an occasional excuse some used to explain while they were there in the woods), or relieve their bladders.

While undercover, I stood in an open bathroom stall once when a male entered and stood at the stall door. There was some awkward idle chit-chat. He said that he was afraid that I might be a cop, because they always picked the cute ones. I pretended that I was flattered. He added "I'm not going to touch you." I said the same thing, but the difference was that I meant it. He couldn't resist temptation. He reached out for a light touch of my private area, which quickly resulted in my grabbing his hand, identifying myself as a police officer by lifting my shirt to show my waist-clipped badge, and arresting him for public lewdness. He was visibly shocked, as they all were in this situation.

One of the Park Rangers would sometimes talk extensively with an older male who was very often lingering in the parking lots and the public restrooms in the park, but he could never catch him in any act of public lewdness with another male. Over time this older male became so comfortable talking to this Park Ranger that he was convinced that there was a spark and that they had a connection. One day he made his move on the Park Ranger in the restroom, which resulted in his immediate arrest for public lewdness. He wasn't going to let a simple fact like the Park Ranger was on duty at the time in his Dallas Police Park Ranger uniform get in his way.

I took a suspicious person call that involved a big, strong dude with the nickname of "Nazi". He was well-known to the older veteran officers, but he hadn't been seen in a number of years, I guessed because of a longer-than-usual prison term. He had no warrants, and I commented that I was surprised by his demeanor and cooperation, that he often gave police a problem in the past. He calmly said "I'm getting too old for that shit."

He actually used to often fight the police, laughing and smiling

as he did; I think his strength and resistance to authority gave

him real joy in his younger years, even if he was beaten as

officers were trying to affect his arrest. He proudly displayed

those bruises then like a badge of courage from his fearless

police scuffles.

That may have been the last time that any of us ever had any

contact with him.

---

911 operators are supposed to screen callers and weed out

the ridiculous nonsense, but somehow I was going to a call at a

woman's apartment because a maintenance man had put a hex

on all of her appliances. She was waiting outside for me and

informed me that I may want to put on a mask because the

smell was so bad; I sensed that she was mentally unstable so I

told her that I would manage. She pointed at some white

powder just outside her door and proudly stated that was so

she could see their footprints when they returned to her

apartment. Ingenious. She was wearing rubber gloves, a

hairnet, and a surgical mask and warned me again of how bad it

was inside, so I started to think that I would be overwhelmed by

an intense odor. Instead, when she opened the door, I could

only smell citric freshness. Her apartment was empty except for

a twin sized mattress on the floor and a few clothes. Her carpet

was wet in spots where she had cleaned it, her counter and

linoleum floor were still wet from cleaning. Despite it being

clean by all appearances and odor-free, she was spraying

disinfectant spray every few steps. She opened a cabinet and

pointed to some "funk" by the hinge, but I saw nothing. She

told me that she had called the manager and that she wasn't

going to put up with it anymore—she was moving out. The

manager could only hope.

A man was wandering in and out of the street. I arrived to

see that the Fire Department was already there. The suspect vital signs were fine, he was just intoxicated. I handcuffed him,

shoved my left hand into his left pant pocket to search him, and

realized too late that he had urinated on himself. I pulled out a

wet wad of crumpled bills, but didn't look inside them, not

wanting to expose my ungloved hands too his urine any longer

than necessary. Well, at Detox they found a small baggie of

marijuana inside the urine-soaked currency during their search,

so we went to the county jail instead for a possession of

marijuana charge.

The manager of a government owned assisted living complex

and one of her residents met me two blocks away from the

complex. Five days earlier this resident sold his recliner to a

neighbor for $50, but two days after that, the neighbor called

back and said that he needed that $50 back because he needed

to buy a $100 shotgun. Then with that shotgun he was going to

kidnap the manager and force her to drive him to the V.A.

Hospital where he would kill the doctors that condemned him

to die by diagnosing him with AIDS. After that carnage, he

would kill the manager and then commit suicide. He might have

just been blowing off some steam, but this wasn't a call that we

could view with indifference. We went back to the complex and

escorted the manager to her office, where she promptly locked

her door and called to hire an armed security guard at our

behest. Meanwhile, we went upstairs to make contact with the

misdirected rage lunatic. He had posted a medical notice on his

door to warn all visitors that he had the Epstein Barr virus and

mononucleosis. After several knocks a neighbor directly across

the hall opened his door and informed us that his friend wasn't

home and was already at the V.A. Hospital. He added that

though our suspect was depressed and angry and sometimes

threatened to kill those that gave him any trouble, that he

didn't actually have any weapons in his apartment. We alerted

the manager who had already arranged for constables to evict

the absent tenant. I called the V.A. Hospital and spoke to

security to alert them of his name and description in the event

that his empty threats were orchestrated. Our suspect had

enough to worry about medically but he would soon find out

that his unrestrained and threatening mouth had caused him to

be among the indigent and homeless.

Auto theft detectives had a number of patrol officers meet

with them to discuss an operation that was about to happen. A

truckload of "Crotch rocket" motorcycles had been stolen, and a

large group of these were believed to be at a nearby Sonic. We

all converged on the parking lot and the many riders were quick

to flee, going over curbs and between bushes. We only snagged

a few from their MC's, and they were indeed stolen. Eventually,

nearly all of them were recovered.

Occasionally police receive calls about drugs possibly being

sold from a home or apartment. If I was the officer doing the

talking or "Knock and Talk", as it is known, I would tell them

exactly why I was at their front door, but say it nonchalantly and

add "I know that it sounds ridiculous." This would disarm them and they wouldn't always perceive me as a threat. I would play it off like if they would let us take a quick walk around inside, we could put this rumor to rest really quickly and be back on our way. Most of the time we were invited inside to take a quick look around when they had nothing to hide. Other times, the man at the door would say no, or even no, you're not coming in here without a warrant. That would give us a reason to be suspicious and that was when we knew to notify Narcotics with a Drug House report.

An officer that I worked with at White Rock Lake was flagged down about some young males in a car being suspicious. They were driving slowly through parking lots and stopping at times to casually look inside vehicles while standing next to or near them. These guys were certainly car burglars, and the officer summoned me to cover him. He made a traffic stop, and I told him that I would contact our Deployment Unit. They wore plain clothes and watched suspicious people and vehicles to hopefully catch crooks in the act of committing a crime which was when they would call in the uniformed officers to swoop in and make the arrest(s). We had to stall the suspects while we waited for them to arrive. I told one of them that had a common name a lie that someone by that name was wanted for murder out of Austin. He smiled and said that it wasn't him, and I smiled too to reassure him and put his friends at ease and commented that as soon as I found out in a few more minutes we would cut them loose. A Deployment officer informed us by radio that they had arrived and were in position and would take it from there. I cut our suspects loose after telling them that the guy with the murder warrant was 6'4", 270 pounds, much larger than he was.

Later that day I found out that these suspects had been followed to a large shopping mall parking lot. As a professional courtesy, the deployment officers phoned that city police agency to inform them of their surveillance. A rambunctious uniformed officer from that city had come uncomfortably close to the area and was seen by the suspects from a good distance.

That was all that it took. The suspects were sufficiently spooked

that they ended their vehicle burglary before it began. The

undercover officer told me that it was so close to happening

that one of the suspects had actually stepped out of the vehicle

and wrapped a towel around his hand to punch out a car

window when they suddenly halted and fled the scene.

Some City of Garland undercover officers had located a

suspect in Dallas and requested assistance from some of our

uniformed officers to approach him. I was the only officer that

volunteered. The suspect was working on his motorcycle in his

apartment complex, and had warrants for Burglary, Prohibited

Weapon (for pipe bombs), Components of Bomb, and was

thought to be personally armed and dangerous. I was told that

he would probably fight to elude capture, but that they would

be watching me and would assist me should that happen. I

pulled up, exited my squad car and ordered the suspect to the pavement at gunpoint. He complied and was handcuffed. He was surprised that I had been informed that he was dangerous, and smilingly said "I'm not a fighter and would never hurt anybody" (yet he built pipe bombs).

A woman got involved in her first interracial relationship. After a couple months she believed that their relationship was shaky. She hired a P.I. to uncover some of her boyfriend's past, as she was uncomfortable knowing so little about him. She couldn't shrug off the feeling that he had something evil hiding in his past. She discovered that he had been to prison, was on parole, and had stalked a previous girlfriend. The woman was frightened and broke off their relationship by ignoring his calls. Two weeks later, he confronted her at her mailbox to question why she wouldn't return his calls and why she was mad at him, and she informed him of her decision.

Days later, the ex-boyfriend showed up at her workplace and unashamedly told her "You better watch your back! I'm never going to let you go! Nobody can have you! I know how to get

to you through family and friends. I'll kill everybody to get to

you!"

Weeks later, the woman had the chance to get away from

Dallas and leave the stress of dealing with this obsessive ex-

boyfriend behind her by going on a long-planned trip to Denver.

When her flight arrived, she was shocked and shivered in fear

when he approached her from inside the airport, smiling and

acting like everything was normal. He had remembered her trip

and had driven 14 hours to meet her there. He was far from

normal. I made a stalking offense report for her.

A woman called 911 after a long-time friend had called her to

say that he was depressed and had slashed his wrists.

Paramedics and another officer were waiting at his locked door

when I arrived. The complex office was closed, so a fireman

kicked in the front door and we searched the apartment for the

suicidal occupant. He wasn't there. Perhaps he went for

medical attention, or perhaps he wanted to dramatize his (alleged) suicide. On the table we found a marriage certificate, a plastic bride and groom wedding cake decoration and a two-page suicide note with what appeared to be two blood drops almost precisely on the center of the first page. There were no blood drops anywhere else in the apartment. The letter explained how he was grief-stricken that his marriage hadn't worked out, and emphasized his ever-lasting love for his ex-wife. It was a depressing and believable suicide note, until the bottom of the second page. Our sense of urgency and his level of depression were considerably diminished when we read: "P.S. I sold the TV for $75 so I could get something to eat and go fix my car."

A woman and two men--one being her son-- decided they wanted to steal a car in the parking lot. A window was down far enough that they could unlock and enter the vehicle without causing any damage. The ignition switch was already broken and was cranked several times, but the car wouldn't start. The

criminals popped the hood, and gave the battery a jump so that

now the engine was running. The woman put the car into drive

and tried to drive away, but a bad transmission kept her from

moving. She pressed the accelerator further so that the engine

was racing, but the car wouldn't budge. The owner stepped

outside and confronted these suspects, but they ignored him.

He went back inside and phoned the police. We showed up and

as we were talking to him, the woman that tried to steal his car

returned, but we could not arrest her for Unauthorized Use of a

Motor Vehicle. She had entered the car, started the engine, put

the car in drive, tried to drive off, and obviously had the intent

to steal it. The problem was that according to the Texas Penal

Code, the definition of a "Vehicle" is "that which may be or is

being propelled." The faulty transmission made that

impossible. She escaped the felony charge by a loophole, but

went to jail for ticket warrants.

An undercover officer found an occupied stolen vehicle, and

when three squad cars were behind it--including me--we turned

on our overhead lights to make the traffic stop. The stolen

vehicle began to slow and started to pull over, but then rapidly

accelerated. The chase was on! As the last car, I was calling the

chase on the radio because the second car was a Sergeant. As

the speed increased, naturally we were further apart from each

other for safety in case of a quick stop. As I turned into an

apartment complex, I saw the passenger run from the stopped

stolen car. The sirens were still wailing from the two now

empty police cars in front of me. I bolted from my car to pursue

the passenger, and ran through a breezeway thinking it open at

the end so I could turn and see the passenger who was running

on the other side of the building. No such luck, it became a

dead end, and I had to make a u-turn. Weapon drawn, I quickly

looked into several ground level balconies, hoping to get lucky

and find my suspect. I ran across a parking lot into a grassy

tree-shaded area between buildings. A passerby pointed to

help me out, and I could now see the passenger about to go up a flight of stairs. I yelled "HEY!" to get his attention as I ran toward him. He halted, and I heard another officer yell "FREEZE!" The frightened passenger complied and when I reached him, I ordered him to the ground. As I pushed him against a wall and tugged down on the collar of his sweater, he went to the sidewalk. His name was later confirmed from fingerprinting, and he went to Jail for Evading and unpaid tickets. The stolen vehicle smelled like marijuana, but none was found. The driver escaped for now, but fingerprints were obtained from a glass drink bottle on the driver side floorboard.

A young man tried to steal three raunchy, erotic movie collections from an electronics store but was caught by their Loss Prevention officers. He told me that he couldn't help himself, and that he had to take them. At the jail he saw the nurse for an obsessive/compulsive disorder.

A woman had just dropped off her son at school, and was driving home with her second husband sitting beside her. She reached over to turn down the radio which caused an immediate reaction by him shouting at her, punching her on her mouth causing a bloody, swollen lip, and telling her that he would kill her. She called police from her apartment, and said that the last few weeks the suspect had been verbally abusive and she believed that he had not been taking his medication. He was hateful to us too, not providing us with any book-in sheet information, just calling us "Honky" or "White mother-fuckers." He was arrested for Family Violence Assault, and saw the county jail nurse for his schizophrenia.

A Deployment (undercover) officer noticed a vehicle that had two different license plates, and asked for a uniformed officer to make a traffic stop. The two men inside stopped in a parking space and exited the vehicle just moments before I pulled up behind them to turn on my lights for a traffic stop. When I asked them for ID, neither had any. The other uniformed officer arrived. I searched the vehicle for marijuana as I had smelled it in the air just after they had closed their car doors, but none was found. I asked the driver again if he had any ID on him at all, anything with his name on it. He held his hands up in the air and said "No, you can look." I did. He was right, he had no ID on him, but he did have two baggies of marijuana inside his left shirt pocket that I found. He was cuffed and taken to jail, and his passenger went to jail for ticket warrants.

One of the license plates was the old expired tag and hadn't been removed.

I received a call about a man holding a gun inside his bedroom. I arrived to see that he was still holding the gun in his hand and I ordered him at gunpoint to drop it. He did so. The pistol had been unloaded and empty. For my safety, I patted him down for any additional weapons but only found two cooking spoons and an unused syringe in his left pant pocket.

He told me that he cooked a prescription drug because he found out that it had opiates in it and he wanted to get high. Having made no threats to harm himself or others, he was left with the three other people in the house who now knew that he didn't have any ammunition for his pistol. He received a ticket for possession of drug paraphernalia, which was confiscated.

A woman hadn't seen her nephew for a year and was not aware of his psychological problems when she agreed to let him stay at her home during his probation. The nephew was recently released and had been staying with her for just four days but she'd had enough already. He yelled sporadically at the top of his lungs for no reason, opened doors to stare at her while she was dressing or undressing, he enjoyed destroying things, heard voices and carried on conversations when no one was there, and urinated in her car. She couldn't find any of her aerosol cans because her nephew was hoarding them for his olfactory pleasures to get high from the inhalants. She had him garden to keep him busy, but once he got up and ran suddenly because he thought he was being chased by George Washington (he managed to elude capture). We met the aunt at the end of her street in her car because she was afraid to be alone with her nephew because of his outbursts and mental instability. We went to the house and the nephew was calm, saying he was about to leave to go see his probation officer within an hour. In private, I told the Aunt to pack his few things outside the door after he left with a note on the door and to lock him out. If she wanted she could leave him a little money to help him out and induce him to leave and possibly convince him to stay gone.

A woman was expecting a friend so she answered the door without looking to see who it was. It wasn't her friend. Three suspects burst inside and forced her to her bedroom where she was duct taped. Two were armed with handguns. One of the suspects raped her, while another went for her safe, and the other looked in her house for valuable property to steal. The

expected friend arrived at her front door, was dragged inside by

the suspects, beat up, duct taped, and beat up some more.

When the suspects were ready to leave, they threatened to kill

the woman and man if they called police. The female went to a

small hospital but was told that they didn't have any rape exam

kits (a statewide shortage actually existed at this time). She

reconsidered what she was doing and didn't follow through

with her needed examination nor did she make a police report.

She only phoned police after her son happened to fly in from

North Carolina for a visit not long afterward. Through tears, she

confided in him and told him of her sexual assault. He

encouraged her with his love and emotional support to involve

the police.

I was sitting in my police cruiser inside a park when I was

approached by a homeless woman who asked me if I could give

her a ride. She had a quarrel with her boyfriend and wanted to get away. I gave her a ride alright—straight to Detox for Public Intoxication.

I was going to meet a co-worker for lunch in 15 minutes. Worried that I might get a call and ruin my lunch plans, I decided to mark out on a traffic stop until lunch time. I saw a girl go past me in the opposite direction without wearing her seatbelt. I made a u-turn to follow and saw that she was driving 45 in a 30 zone. She turned right at a stop sign without stopping or signaling. I did a traffic stop and she had no DL, no insurance, and an expired license plate. That's seven possible tickets. A computer DL check also showed a ticket warrant from a Dallas Suburb. Luckily for her, I was hungry so I didn't want to "jail traffic" her for her seven traffic violations and her ticket warrant, and then tow her car. I wrote two citations, sent her on her way, and resumed my trip for lunch.

A woman from the same apartment complex babysat for three children, aged 5, 3, and 2 while the mother went out to a bar, telling her that she would return shortly after 2 a.m. when the bar closed. At 9 a.m. the sitter left the children with a neighbor who happened to stop by to visit as she did every morning. The neighbor stayed and received a phone call from the mother at a hotel about 20 miles away; the mother had gone there with a man she had met at the bar and was just now calling to report her whereabouts, more than 9 hours after she should've been home. Her neglect earned her a Child Protective Services Referral, and CPS would be monitoring her and making occasional unannounced visits.

I was driving through a pharmacy parking lot and did a license plate check on my computer. The vehicle returned as stolen, so I swung around to get behind it, turning on my emergency lights. A pleasant, well-mannered mother was driving, and her two pretty teenaged daughters were in the car with her. I informed them that the vehicle showed to be stolen.

They were surprised, but not nervous. Shockingly, the mother's

valid ID returned to a "Known Offender"; she didn't seem the

type. She had been released from prison recently after having

done time for manslaughter for murdering her husband. She

explained that her son had wanted her to have a car when she

was released, so he had bought it for her. The car key still had

the car lot tag attached to it. This was before everyone had a

cell phone, and her son was not at home when we called. The

car lot was closed as it was a Sunday. We recovered the vehicle

as stolen, and towed it to our Auto Pound. The driver had valid

ID, and said that her son had the receipt and a title at home. I

made the report and listed her as the suspect. She might end

up with a U.U.M.V. (Unauthorized Use of Motor Vehicle)

warrant, but not until an Auto Theft detective could do some

research. She and her daughters were released.

In an early morning hour, a girl was driving down the freeway and her headlights illuminated a lawn chair in her lane up ahead. She swerved to avoid hitting it, went off the freeway, hit a short wooden post with the front of her car, then toppled lengthwise once end over end and landed on the car top. Amazingly, she was unhurt. She just unbuckled her seatbelt as she hung upside down, climbed out, and was waiting for us when we arrived.

An ex-Navy Seal spoke to me at White Rock Lake and wanted me to know that he and a film crew would be there hours later to film and photograph him as a Navy Seal emerging out of the water with his unloaded weapon to be used in promotional materials and on his website to promote his new business. He wondered if there could be a police presence just at one small parking lot with a pier so as not to startle lake users and have someone call 911. I alerted my Sergeant who agreed, and I contacted another officer for the occasion. A man of his word, he told us that he would deliver each of us a shirt from his business to thank us, and he later did.

I wrote a no parking ticket to a woman who didn't think that I was being fair and became argumentative. She had parked along a road with several "No Parking Anytime" signs, but the nearest sign was five yards in front of her car. She had parked between two signs. Using what she thought was logic, she tried to reason with me and said "The sign is up there and I'm back here."

I was driving slowly alongside businesses in a shopping center when two teenaged males who were talking on my left caught my eyes. They had been smiling until they spotted me, which raised a red flag making them suspicious. They both had a surprised look on their faces and one of them suddenly closed one hand into a fist. I stopped my police cruiser and walked over to them. Both were frozen and obviously scared, and one of them scrambled off quickly. He was not the one I thought to be most suspicious, so I let him flee. I asked the remaining 16-year-old what he had in his hand. He opened it to reveal a joint and said "a marijuana cigarette sir." I handcuffed him, and he informed me that he had just found it on the ground and picked it up. I searched him incident to his arrest and found a clear plastic baggie of marijuana in a pants pocket. He declared that marijuana wasn't his either. It belonged to his brother, because he was wearing his brother's pants that day. Ha! Thanks for clearing that up. I called his older brother who was an adult and told him that I was transporting his younger brother to the Juvenile Justice Center for having possession of marijuana. He was incredulous because his brother had just been arrested for the same thing two months earlier, and this incident violated his probation.

A terminated convenient store employee decided to get his revenge on the owner by driving his vehicle through the front of the store.   His vehicle got stuck and he was still present when we arrived after being dispatched on the call. He was arrested for felony criminal mischief.

A woman's apartment was burglarized. She had some property stolen, but peculiarly nothing was taken from the usually targeted bedroom where she and most people kept some real valuables. It wasn't a mystery. The entire apartment had the strong odor of used kitty litter, and the acrid foul cat urine wreaked the worst at the location of the litter box—in her bedroom. A definite man deterrent, be it burglar or invited guest.

A partner and I were driving through a motel parking lot, checking registrations on the computer to search for stolen vehicles. An 11-year-old pickup truck showed to be stolen. Even before we left the parking lot, this vehicle backed up and drove into a different parking space. She had just arrived to rent a room and had briefly parked near the office, and now she was driving nearer her room location. We swung around behind her, popped on our lights, and extracted her for an arrest. She claimed that she didn't know the vehicle was stolen. Off to jail she went for the stolen truck, for drug paraphernalia found in her purse, and a make-up-kit which included a full syringe of liquid crack cocaine diluted with lemon juice.

About one mile from my station, I found a large green rectangular metal sign for "Kilgore, TX" lying flat on the road and placed it in the back seat of my cruiser. It must have been some kid prank. I placed it outside our police station for what at the time was the storage area for oversized property. I'm sure the town was happy to get their sign back, but someone had to drive 120 miles to retrieve it.

As late as the 1990's, there was no "overdraft protection" for bank and credit union customers. If someone didn't have enough money in their account and a check "bounced", or wrote what was termed a "hot check", that person would have an IBC (Issuance of a Bad Check) warrant(s) if the intended recipient couldn't get paid and filed on them. I arrested a young college aged girl once for that very thing and she missed an airline flight that she had a few hours later.

In 1994, Dallas was one of the cities in the USA where soccer games of the World Cup Finals were to be played. Several hundred Dallas Officers parked in a large lot near the Cotton Bowl each morning, then were all bussed over to the stadium. We had riot gear, and had been trained to handle issues that might arise from soccer fan hooliganism, especially from the English. The Dallas PD Intelligence Unit had said that they doubted the hooligans would test Dallas Police Officers because we had a reputation for professionalism and taking care of business. They were right; outside of the occasional drunk or minor scuffle, we had no serious issues.

An officer from the previous shift had been shot in the leg, and another officer was able to use our newly issued tourniquets to stem the bleeding. Because of all the police cars present at the crime scene, it was decided that me and a few others who were the first to arrive on the next shift would go to the scene and shuffle some cars back for what was sure to be a car shortage if we didn't. We only knew the basics of what happened and played no role in the police shooting. As we waited on scene, a sergeant pointed to elucidate, and I was standing next to her at the time. That was all it took for a news photographer to capture an "action" shot. We made the newspaper the next day.

I had a call about a dog constantly barking inside an apartment. The unit turned out to be vacant, and everything was gone, except for a friendly Pitbull dog that was on a leash that the resident(s) left behind. He was probably adopted by someone after Animal Control retrieved him.

There were a few other times when I came across dogs that had been abandoned not in an apartment, but in a park. One abandoned dog kept looking for its owner and ran with every car that passed. When it became aware that the driver was not its owner, it returned to the spot where it had been dumped. Another dog was left tied to a tree at the lake in a grassy area and had a bowl of water, left near a dog park. Both were rescued by Animal Control after I summoned them.

A woman had been estranged from her husband for several months, but didn't actually think that he was dating another woman much less having one live with him. She went to his apartment and banged on his front door and wouldn't go away. We arrived and ended up bringing her to a bus stop so that she could go home. She had told us that we needed to take her to jail, but we didn't have a reason. Thirty minutes later, another call came out from the same location. It is customary and expected that if possible, when this happens, the original officers should respond to take care of business to avoid a third call. We returned to find her and her husband arguing on the sidewalk. We instructed the man to go back inside his apartment, and he complied. Several minutes later, the man returned because he was concerned that his wife had already or might damage his vehicle. The woman ran toward her husband and said "I hate you! I hate you!", threw her purse in his face, then slapped him on his back, shoulder, and arms while he tried to fend off her strikes by raising his arms. We pulled her away and handcuffed her for M/C Assault Family Violence.   She again told us that she needed to go jail, because if she didn't, she would be back out there again tonight. When she was placed in the squad car and realized that she actually was going

to jail this second time, she changed her mind and pleaded with

us to just take her home because she learned her lesson and

she'd never return again. Too late.

My rookie and I noticed two Texas Parks & Wildlife Officers

each preparing a boat to test on the lake, as spring was

underway and they wanted to be prepared for a season of use.

I climbed into my friend's boat while my rookie boarded the

other, and we motored out to the middle of the lake. Our boat

sputtered and stopped, and we couldn't get it restarted.

Twenty seconds later, the other boat noticed our stoppage,

then returned alongside of us to help and stopped their engine.

We couldn't get our motor started, so the other boat would

have to tow us to shore. But, they couldn't get their motor

started either. We all refused to have the fire department

launch their boat to come rescue us, so we all paddled the

couple hundred yards to shore, thankful it was a small Dallas Lake and not the 35 square mile lake over which our patrol division also had jurisdiction.

A female customer was second in line at a 7-11 when several males stepped in front of her to be with their friend, as they were daily customers who always paid together in one transaction. Unaware of this, the woman became incensed that this had happened, and questioned the female clerk behind the counter why she didn't do anything about it, and that she didn't think it was very good customer service. The clerk focused on quickly finishing the transaction and did not respond. Feeling ignored, the female customer blurted out "White whore! Mother fucking bitch!" then started to walk out. The clerk reciprocated and replied by hurling the insult "Black bitch!" The female customer left the store, and soon afterward the males followed, having completed their group purchase. The female customer stepped back into the store and shoved the clerk into

a metal display rack, which caused a laceration to her left

eyebrow. The female suspect then pulled the clerk backwards,

causing her to fall onto the floor. She struck her head on the

tile and got a quick bruise. I received the disturbance call from

just two blocks away and when I arrived, the suspect had the

front door open and was yelling back at the clerk, who had gone

back behind the counter to attend to other customers. The

other officer arrived, and I handcuffed the suspect after

confirming the M/A Assault by watching the store videotapes.

The suspect's car was towed.

The judge who had this case assigned to his court could not

view the videotape evidence on the city video playback

equipment, and would have to view the video in the office of

the offense location. He phoned me and asked me about it,

informing me that before sentencing the arrestee, he wanted to

view the evidence. I encouraged him to do that, as the

victim/clerk had put up no resistance and was outmatched by

the much larger defendant.

Weeks later, the Judge gave me a courtesy call and told me

that he finally had made the trip to the store to watch the tape.

He agreed with my perspective and commented that the clerk

had been "tossed around like a ragdoll."

After receiving an alarm call one night, another officer sent

us a one-word message on our computer: "Boo!" He knew that

the address was a funeral home. We arrived to find a partly

open front door with the alarm sounding. We entered with

weapons drawn to conduct a building search. A dead body was

lying on a metal table in a very cool room. We checked all of

the rooms, and the inside of open and closed caskets in case a

live burglar had the courage to hide inside. No one was found,

it was just another false alarm as are most.

The Mortician arrived to secure his business and to ascertain

that nothing had been stolen. Conversing with him, he

mentioned that he inherited the business from his father, whom he himself had embalmed two years earlier. He thanked us and told us that he couldn't do what we did for a living. Back at ya buddy.

During early morning daylight hours on a weekend, a few officers and I were trying to drive and maneuver and park to channel a deer back into a wooded area. No one knew if it was a pet from somebody's yard, or if it came out of the woods, but there was no nearby woodland. The best we could do was direct it to a narrow-wooded creek area that ran for miles, where it escaped but by this time with a dog catcher net over its head.

We received a call about a suspect hunkering down inside a vehicle each time that somebody walked past him. Another caller reported that he had been sleeping in the car for more than three hours. Prior to our arrival we called and the witnesses told us the man had just driven off going westbound.

We still found him sleeping inside the car, the same reported by

the witnesses who also identified him as the driver. The

arrestee claimed that he didn't know that the vehicle had been

stolen, despite a Philips head screwdriver sticking out of the

missing ignition lock, and a missing radio. Coming down from

some drug (meth?), all he wanted to do on the way to jail and at

the jail was sleep.

A maintenance man/porter of a small property with just a

few businesses was angry because several times in the previous

two weeks in early morning daylight, somebody had dumped 30

or 40 pounds of catfish heads, entrails, tails, and bones on the

parking lot. The location was poorly chosen because the

violator could've dumped the fish scrap across the street in the

woods for some wild animals to devour instead. Our caller was

incensed that he had to clean up the stinking mess. Getting

lucky this day, he saw the suspect do the illegal dumping in the act and wrote down the vehicle license plate number as the suspect drove away. I contacted the county's Illegal Dump Team sergeant with the case number of the report that I made. Weight of the refuse determined the severity of the charge, so this was a felony.

I stopped a man for speeding. He apologized, saying that he was late for work and also said that he had been out of the country for a while and his DL had expired. That was an understatement; it had expired 5 years earlier and his original driver's license number had been reissued and was now someone else's ID card number. I wrote him a ticket for an expired DL, but not for speeding. I also wrote him a note for his boss on a sheet of paper that he gave me. It read "To who it may concern: Please excuse Charles for being late to work today. Try as he may, try as he might, his rushing to work did not escape the notice of the Dallas Police Department," then signed and dated it. He was a nice guy. I didn't mind.

Many years ago I stopped a car as it pulled into a Kroger Store parking space. I had checked the license plate and two people who had been driving the vehicle had ticket warrants. The guy stepped out of the vehicle and was 6'2", 240 lbs. He had a bit of vitriol in his voice when he asked me "What did I do?" I told him that as soon as he showed me his driver's license and proof of insurance, I would tell him. Reaching into his pocket he handed me his DL, but said that he had borrowed the vehicle and couldn't access the locked glove compartment for the insurance card. Appearing to be a gang member, he wore loose-fitting clothes and a doo rag, but had effeminate mannerisms. I was perplexed by the unisex aspect. I actually didn't know if I was looking at a man or a woman. The DL check showed that the motorist was a female, but I started wondering if maybe it wasn't her DL. I asked for the birthday, address, and number of the DL, but she knew all three. I commented to her that the picture looked a bit different than she did. She smiled and said that she was a transexual. Deciphering the puzzled

look on my face, she asked "You know what a transexual is,

don't you?" I replied yes, but I was actually thinking

transvestite at the time. Still not convinced that I knew (I

didn't), he clarified "I have titties like a woman and I've had

surgery so that I look like a woman down there." That was a

first for me. I gave him/her the names of the two people that

had warrants, and sent him/her on his/her way.

I had pulled into a lake parking lot when I was flagged down

by a man who wanted to know where he and about four other

vehicles could bring their children to a playground at the lake. I

had them follow me for a couple of miles and re-entered the

lake area to show them. I pulled to the side of the road, and

one of the wives on the passenger side of one of the vehicles

smiled and said thank you. I smiled back at the pretty woman

and said "You're Welcome." She continued by asking if she

could take a picture with me and I agreed with a "Sure". The vehicles all parked and we all stepped outside. The friendly

woman walked over to the side of my police car, and as we put

an arm around each other's back, her father took the picture.

We were both smiling. Several other teenaged girls and women

from the entourage were watching, smiling and laughing at

their friend's willingness to have a photo with me. Seeing the

irony, and being charming with a great sense of humor, the

happy woman made the observation "Normally you are

following us, but today we followed you." It was a great

positive public relations contact for me and these Muslims.

The most popular recreational spot in Dallas is White Rock

Lake. At times when families go for a bike ride, the children ride

too far ahead. Sometimes the parents rightly panic when they

lose sight of them and can't find them. We were called once by

parents and because their two children were under 10 years

old, we looked for them until they were found. I enlisted the

support of other officers and our helicopter for the search. The kids were actually found waiting for their parents at their car, having circled most of the 9 miles of the lake on the bike path themselves.

I had a call which involved a female motorist whose ex-husband was sideswiping her on the freeway. She exited and went to a drive-thru, where some witnesses had the suspect blocked. I was driving that way and had to stop at a red light. Now information came over the radio that the woman had fled the restaurant drive-thru and was presently near the intersection where I was located. The light went green, and I started driving slowly with my head on a swivel searching for my complainant. It was bumper-to-bumper traffic, and a sudden chain reaction stop for the slow-moving cars happened in front of me. By the time that I noticed and hit my brake, I had already struck the rear bumper of the car to my front. The speed was probably only 10 to 15 mph, but certainly enough to cause whiplash. My airbag deployed, and I choked and coughed from the air bag powder. I stepped out to check on the condition of the woman driving the vehicle that I struck. She looked okay, just a little shaken. A man approached and asked me if I had an ambulance coming. I thought that he might be her husband or boyfriend. I asked her if she wanted an ambulance, and he encouraged her and me to start one. I ordered one from the dispatcher while back inside my police cruiser. Walking back, I saw that the man was now in her car sitting on the back seat directly behind her. He was holding his hands on the sides of her head, commanding her to stay still and not move her head. He identified himself to me; he was an injury attorney. I knew at that moment that I was going to be named in a lawsuit, and eventually I was.

Either that day or the next, I went to the hospital with a sergeant to visit the female motorist who was checked into a room. The minor accident had caused little damage to her vehicle, and it was obviously my fault. Still, I was advised to fight that instinct to apologize, that we were only going as a courtesy to see how she was doing. Her icy disgust about our being in her hospital room was palpable; our short visit was extremely awkward.

She sued me and the City of Dallas, claiming headaches, memory loss, loss of income and loss of clients. I had to provide a videotaped deposition in the presence of her lawyer and city attorneys. Though I was told the city would defend the lawsuit, I believe there was likely a settlement.

I went inside a McDonalds to get some lunch and noticed a teen male (who turned out to be 14) also standing in line. I asked him why he wasn't in school. He told me that he missed the bus and that his uncle was coming to get him. I told him that after we purchased our lunch that I was going to take him back to school. The kid received his meal and proceeded to walk out the door. I bolted toward him as the door was opening and grabbed him by the back of his collar, reminding him that he was going to school with me. I handcuffed him, and had to steer him to my police cruiser by firmly holding one of his arms.

Along the way, the truant told me that he wasn't going

anywhere, that he was going to talk to his dad first. I responded

by saying his dad could pull him out of school if he so wanted.

Now the 7th grader was refusing to sit in the vehicle, so I had to

push him off balance to get him seated and buckled. As I took

him to his Middle School he was on a tireless tirade of rhetoric

"You Mother-Fucker! You can't tell me what to do! No one can

do that but my dad! Mother-fuckin' punk!" (in fairness, earlier

in the ride I had said that he was nothing but a punk). His

mouth abated as we got closer to his school, but he still warned

me that I should wait to see what happened when I took the

cuffs off, that he wasn't afraid of me, that I had better take the

cuffs off when he told me to, that he would just run out the

front door (I guess his uncle wasn't picking him up), as well as

some unintelligible mutters that I couldn't understand. Upon

arrival, he didn't want to get out but I reminded him that I had

his food and he could eat it in the office. He stepped out and I

guided him to the office. At one time he tried to pull away to go down the hallway instead, but I pulled him back and sat him inside the school office. School officials arrived, including the principal who the truant obviously respected. The truant sought sympathy from him and told him that I couldn't tell him what to do. The shocked principal told him that I was a police officer, that I was an authority figure and that he had to listen to me. That made an impact on the kid and he calmed completely. I removed his handcuffs, and I left him to be processed by the school.

I heard that the kid just walked out of the school an hour later. This kid with an attitude would probably be no stranger to the criminal justice system as an adult.

Intelligence officers requested that some uniformed officers meet them in a restaurant parking lot. Being just blocks away, I volunteered. They told us that at the end of the block, a suspect named Thompson was at a Cadillac Dealership. The uniformed officers waited in position not far away for the signal.

"Go! Go! Go!" from an undercover officer watching the suspect

and his friends. They were leaving in a different Cadillac and

had to wait for a light that just turned red. Our approach from

their right was perfectly shielded because there happened to be

a white van in the lane to the suspect vehicle right. Racing

toward them, I was the lead police car. I pulled in front of the

stopped white van and turned a hard left, causing my car to

fishtail to my right. My car stopped at a 45-degree angle to the

front of the stopped suspect car as if I had been a stunt driver. I

jumped from my car with pistol in hand. The suspect vehicle

had all tinted windows. I opened the driver door and there was

a female at the wheel. I ordered "Get your hands up! Get your

hands up!" She did, but then the car began to lurch forward

because it was still in drive. The passenger reached over and

put the gear shift in park. Other officers were now also at the

car and opened doors shouting "Get your hands up! Get out of

the car!" We handcuffed two males and two females, and

placed them all in separate police cruisers so any false story

could not be collaborated among them. They had just paid cash for the Cadillac and were taking it for a short drive before they returned to the car that they had used to get there. I found a pistol in that car which was dusted for latent fingerprints. The pistol was probably used to rob several people, and possibly to have shot someone just days earlier. Since all were Aggravated Robbery suspects and potentially very dangerous, two uniformed officers accompanied each suspect on the drive downtown to speak with detectives.

The next day I learned that about twenty Aggravated Robbery offenses were cleared from their capture. Thompson and his gang were one of the 10 most wanted criminals in the State of Texas.

A forgery suspect was at a bank. He had attempted to cash a counterfeit check, and the tellers became suspicious and verified from the check owner that the suspect was unknown to him. The suspect became impatient and wanted the forged check and his ID back, but was told to wait just a bit longer. I was already on my way there from a 911 call. The suspect twice

stepped outside of his car and yelled at the tellers on the other

side of the drive-thru glass demanding the return of his ID. The

bank phoned again to ask officers to hurry, because the 42-

year-old suspect was now trying to get over the teller counter

from the inside. We activated our overhead lights and siren,

and I hustled inside the bank just as the suspect was walking

toward me to exit the front door. He was subdued with no

resistance and went to jail for the felony Forgery.

I was always an officer that would do as he was told and

accepted every assignment. At some point your superiors

realize that and rather than take some gaff and pushback from

other officers, even though to be fair it was their turn for some

undesirable duty, they would just assign you. For a second day

in a row, the Dallas Police Department had to provide police

officers as school crossing guards (you read that right) because

the city hadn't prepared adequately for the new school year

and was late processing new hires for those positions. I was

disgusted. I radioed my element number to the dispatcher,

along with the on-air comment of "because of somebody's

incompetence and ineptitude, I too must be a school zone

crossing guard at…." I wasn't about to take this in stride. Many

officers laughed at my boldness and defiance , but one sergeant

was told to pull the audio tape from communications and I was

written up.

  The police substitutions for crossing guard was short lived,

and I never had to do it again. It had made the newspaper and

citizens were also rightly disturbed by the misuse of their

taxpayer dollars.

  I pulled a car over for a two-month expired inspection

sticker. The driver pulled into the enclosed fenced area of a car

repair business. He told me that he didn't have any ID, so I told

him to step out of the car; I wanted to ascertain that he didn't

have a wallet in his back pocket. The driver stepped out, placed his hands on top of his car, but then dashed off, running about two hundred yards to a church area. I radioed for cover, and he was found trying to hide by cowering down in tall grass between the side of the church and a fence. He said he ran because he knew that he had a warrant. A check showed that he had a Parole Violation out of TDC (Texas Dept. of Corrections). I called an ambulance for him while he sat in another officer's car because he told us that he felt like he was going to die. He also said that he needed to "take a shit." After assuring us that he was for real, I decided that rather than endure the stench of defecation in the police cruiser all the way to jail that we would let him "drop trousers". We had him step out of the car, and while shielded from view by us and the open car door, he dropped his pants and defecated next to the car while still handcuffed. Shortly after being placed back in the car, he vomited on the back seat. The other officer was extra vigilant and perused through the vomit with a pen looking for ingested drugs; he found none. A 2/3 empty small bottle of Seagram's Extra Dry Gin was found in his car, which would explain his upheaval shortly after his escape run. There were also 24 rounds of .32 caliber ammo found inside his car, but no pistol. Perhaps he flung it during his attempt to elude capture, but we never found it despite an intensive search.

An 18-year-old called 911 from his friend's apartment to report that this friend had stolen his cell phone. An officer assigned to the call phoned this friend, who said that he didn't know anything about the man's stolen phone, but did know that he just drove away in a stolen white Chevy Pickup truck! As I arrived to the apartment complex, the other officer was pulling over the 18-year-old in the presumed stolen truck. I assisted with the arrest. There were no tags on the vehicle which had a broken steering column. I did a VIN check, and found that the vehicle was stolen weeks earlier.

While it was raining and sleeting on a cold April day in 1996, an officer did a traffic stop. He had the motorist DL to check him from inside the police cruiser when the driver suddenly exited his car and fled. The officer soon found out why; the vehicle was stolen. The officer broadcasted his suspect description. His registered address was only a few blocks away from the traffic stop, so another officer and I went to his apartment to look for him. His mother allowed us to search, but he hadn't come home. A passerby found out what the suspect looked like, and told an officer that he had seen the suspect running WB a few minutes earlier. Officers expanded their search perimeters. I drove to a nearby bridge that gave me an elevated panoramic view. My strategy worked. A minute later, through the rain I saw a figure in the distance run by the RR tracks down below. He seemed to have seen me (I was wearing a long yellow rain coat), and he hustled to the fence around a utility yard. A moment later a squad car arrived on the other side of the utility yard. I alerted that unit by radio that a possible suspect had run to the fence on their right side, just south of their location. The rookie immediately got out to scan the area. He and his trainer spotted the suspect and began running toward him. The suspect retreated and dropped to the ground behind the shallow mound that runs along the RR tracks. Hoping that the officers hadn't spotted him and that the pouring rain would cloak his movement, he got up again to run, but the officers noticed and were now again in pursuit. I saw these officers so to save them the trouble of broadcasting and to let them focus solely on their foot pursuit, I broadcasted that those officers were "on the ground" (chasing a suspect by foot), and provided the direction of travel for other officers. I got back in my car and had to drive 100 yards against traffic, the last 50 using my lights and siren to allow passage to safety in the neighborhood. Seconds later the pursuing officers announced that the suspect was in custody. I arrived to exchange high fives and handshakes over the joy of teamwork in making a good well-coordinated arrest.

While driving through a narrow-wooded area at 20-yard intervals, a raccoon crossed in front of me, then a rabbit, then a possum, all in the same direction. Would a coyote have been

next? Not police related other than it occurred on duty, but

that's just weird.

A woman noticed what she believed to be her baby sitter's

stolen car. She followed the brown Buick with a busted out rear

window and called the police. A felony traffic stop was initiated

by two officers, and moments later I arrived and we took the

suspect into custody. Only it wasn't the right car, as neither the

tag nor VIN returned as stolen. I removed the suspect

handcuffs, apologized and shook his hand. Smiling, he said that

he wasn't worried because he knew that he hadn't done

anything wrong. His back window on his brown Buick had just

been busted out, but he hadn't replaced it yet. Maybe the car

color was the wrong shade of brown? Still, a bizarre

coincidence.

I stopped a young woman for a traffic violation. After checking her DL, I returned it to her with a warning, and added that her DL had a large tear in it and that she needed to get a new one because she could actually get a ticket for it.

"I can't get no ticket for that."

"Yes, you can, you can get a ticket for having a mutilated DL."

"You can't write me no ticket for that. You're just making that up. That's not illegal. You must think I'm stupid."

I snatched that DL that was still between her fingers, returned to my car to write the ticket, then returned and made a believer out of her.

Two girls of about 12 ran across three lanes of traffic. At the median, one girl stopped because she thought traffic was too close and coming too fast, but her friend thought that they could make it if they kept running across, so she pulled the hand of her friend. The lead girl who pulled made it across, but her friend whose hand she pulled and had wanted to stop was hit

by a car and killed just two feet behind her. Her impetuous

decision had cost her friend her life.

____

Loyal Readers,

Thank you for your continued support demonstrated by your purchase of DALLAS COP –VOLUME II MORE THAN 400 TRUE SHORT STORIES. By now you surely have a much greater appreciation of police officers on patrol and the many varied encounters they have with the public. You probably are starting to think like a cop and perhaps wished that you should have been one many years ago, or perhaps it isn't too late to become one? Follow your dreams in whatever you decide to do.

 - "Dost thou love life? Then do not squander time, for that is the stuff life is made of." ---Benjamin Franklin

One final DALLAS COP book remains to be published, albeit a slimmed down version. DALLAS COP VOLUME III will be the last book, still full of interesting stories. I hope you have felt like you've been there alongside of me while you read this book and my previous book DALLAS COP. Let your police ride-along continue when you read DALLAS COP VOLUME III.

--Ray Dethloff--